We Need to Talk

Building Trust
When Communicating
Gets Critical

Robien —
Thanks for
the support —
Phillip Van Hooser
1-15-11

PHILLIP VAN HOOSER

We Need To Talk

Published by Dulaney Publishing, Princeton, Kentucky

Library of Congress Control Number: 2010920628

Library of Congress Cataloging-in-Publication Data:
ISBN-13: 978-1-893322-00-4
ISBN-10: 1-893322-00-9
Printed in the United States of America

Interior Illustrations: Kevin VanHooser
Cover and Interior Design: Whitney Campbell, 207-838-0768

Table of Contents

Foreword...vii

Acknowledgements...ix

Chapter 1   Introduction: "I Ain't Gettin' No Stitches" 1

Chapter 2   Everyone Needs A Hero.................................17

Chapter 3   Principle #1: Talk With People.....................................21

Chapter 4   Principle #2: Explain the Process 31

Chapter 5   Principle #3: Tell the Truth 43

Chapter 6   Principle #4: Work for Understanding 55

Chapter 7   Principle #5: Get Others Involved 71

Chapter 8   Principle #6: Do Your Job 83

Chapter 9   Conclusion: What It All Means 91

Foreword

Most of us began learning to pronounce words, and then combine them beginning a few short months after our birth. As time passed, we eventually learned to
form sentences, paragraphs and even stories. By the time we have progressed
through infancy, childhood, adolescence and forward into adulthood, we admittedly have learned many complex life skills. However, expert communication too
often is not one of them. In workplaces, marketplaces, schools, churches and
homes around the world, far too many people spend – even waste – countless
hours talking—but rarely communicating with the efficiency and success they
know they should—and wish they could.

Recognizing the critical importance of face-to-face, person-to-person communication and the effect it can have on personal and professional relationships, I
have invested a significant portion of my life researching, studying, learning,
applying and attempting to master high-powered communication techniques.
Over time, my quest has become a sort of professional obsession. And then, with
no prior warning and seemingly, from out of nowhere, a priceless communication truth that has proven itself universal—arrived in a totally unexpected way.

Since that day, I have shared that practical communication lesson with thousands of professionals around the globe. Many have told me that their ability to
connect and communicate with employees, peers, customers, vendors, constituents,
friends, family members and even foes, has improved markedly as a result of this
6-step, "split chin" communication process.

And to think, it all began with an unplanned trip to a doctor's office.

Are you ready to learn what it takes to communicate more successfully with anyone, anywhere, anytime and under virtually any circumstance? You'll be able to
use these lessons before you've even finished this book.

If so, then just sit back and relax—because I've got a story for you!

Phillip Van Hooser

Acknowledgements

Acknowledgements in books such as this one are commonly disregarded completely by the causal reader. I understand that. But, I also understand that this book is truly the result of the combined efforts, encouragement and support of a number of very special people. There is no way my conscience would allow me to disregard them without so much as a word of recognition.

I will begin by acknowledging the nameless multitude of individuals who, throughout my life and career, have reminded me in innumerable ways of the importance and value of focused one-on-one communication. These people include my parents, friends, teachers, siblings, coaches, spouse and children, not to mention the tens of thousands of professionals I have communicated with during my 30-plus years of business travels. Communication is always easier when done with interested and interesting people. I have had more than my share of both.

Though most of their names have been changed for a variety of reasons, I owe a debt of gratitude to every character that I have written about in the following pages. These are real people. I know them. I liked them—most of them, at least. More importantly, I learned from them. Each one. I believe you will, too.

The very first person I pitched the idea of *We Need To Talk* to was Mac Anderson, founder of Successories and Simple Truths publishing company. From day one, Mac was supportive of the concept and the story from which it grew. His genuine encouragement provided the initial impetus to tackle the writing project that became *We Need To Talk*. I appreciate you, Mac.

Upon hearing that I had begun a new writing project, Sue Jones, a friend and fellow board member at Farmers Bank and Trust Company, Princeton, Kentucky, gave me a key and complete access to her cabin near western Kentucky's famous Barkley Lake. The comfortable, serene setting made for a wonderful writing environment. Sue's unselfish hospitality and friendship allowed the project to move swiftly from concept to reality.

The original illustrations that grace the pages of this book are the work of a talented young artist who just happens to have a great last name. Kevin

VanHooser is a cousin of mine. But, believe me, that's not why his drawings are in this book. Kevin's drawings are in this book because he is exceptionally good at what he does and because I believe his artistic touch make the stories in this book even better. You may not have heard about his work in the past, but I'm betting you will hear about it in the future.

I want to thank a new friend, Whitney Campbell for the work she has done in creating the format and the cover design for this book. Her attention to detail was eclipsed only by her commitment to serving her customers. When writing, designing and publishing a book on communication skills, I think it imperative to work with people with whom it is easy to talk. Whitney is that person, hands down.

I must publicly acknowledge my wife—AGAIN. Almost nothing I have accomplished over the past twenty five years has been done without the capable support, encouragement and love of my wife, Susan. I must admit that too often, at home, I am a better *preacher* than *practitioner* of interpersonal communication techniques. Nevertheless, Susan has the ability to casually overlook my failings and love me anyway.

There's no way I could conclude these acknowledgements without offering a public shout out to my son, Joe. Not that he will be surprised. For almost a quarter century, Joe has served as an almost constant well-spring of material for my professional keynote speeches and training sessions. I have shared literally hundreds of stories, anecdotes, miscues and screw ups, all with Joe as either the hero or villain, depending on the story. Yet, even from a young age, he has accepted the attention—though not asked for or sought out—with the maturity and diplomacy of a man well beyond his years. I'm proud to say to anyone who will listen that Joe is displaying exceptional communication skills himself. Much like the doctor ordered.

Finally, the doc. The doctor you will read about shortly has served as a positive model and a constant inspiration of how working communication can and should be managed both personally and professionally. His skills should be what we all strive for in our interpersonal communication undertakings. Through this book, his memory and example will hopefully live on.

We Need To Talk

1

Introduction

"I Ain't Gettin' No Stitches!"

Just Another Day

The day dawned like every other day. From all outward appearances, this was just one more normal, predictable, chaotic day in the life of a young family. None of us could have predicted the lasting memory that would be made that day—or the value of the lesson learned from it.

My wife, Susan, was busy with her morning routine of feeding, dressing and generally tending to the needs of our two very active pre-school children. Our three-year old son, Joe, lived life in a state of perpetual motion. He had one speed—and it was always set at full throttle. Our one-year old daughter, Sarah, was only slightly more sedate.

On this seemingly normal weekday morning, Susan was in complete control of all matters of the home and of the hour. Like clockwork, resist as they might, the kids would be fed, dressed and ushered next door for a day of fun and activity with their babysitter. With the kids appropriately delivered, Susan's focus would shift to her "day job" which meant she would slip into her professional clothes, before driving downtown to join me at the office of Van Hooser Associates—the speaking and training business we had built together.

I must admit that my role was little more than that of a bit player in this on-going performance of "domestic theatre." I had been instructed months before that the best thing I could do to help keep the wheels of daily progress turning smoothly was to "stay out of the way," "don't stir up the kids," and to let Susan "handle the details." I also learned that if I left for the office early and without great fanfare, it made Susan's job of corralling Joe and Sarah much easier.

So, on this seemingly routine—soon to be anything but—morning, I planted good-bye kisses on Susan, Joe and Sarah, before heading out the door. I thought I was going to work. But, I was actually going to school—communication school. Little did I know that on this particular day, a doctor's office would become my classroom and I, the student.

The Meaning of *It*

As I closed the door behind me and headed for my car, I heard *it*. The "*it*" was a blood-curdling scream coming from inside my own house—and I immediately recognized *it* for what *it* was.

Though kids certainly scream, holler and cry in different ways, at different times and for different reasons, the particular brand of scream I'm referring to is never interpreted to mean, "I'm hungry," "I'm sleepy," "I'm mad," or "I'm tired." The scream I heard that morning can only be interpreted to mean one thing—"I'm hurt!"

And once it is heard by an adult, it means all other bets are off. Whatever the adult might be doing at the moment the scream is heard becomes secondary to the immediate needs of the child. You stop whatever you're doing and you turn your full attention to offering whatever aid might be necessary. In the Van Hooser household, on this particular day that scream announced clearly that a seemingly routine morning had suddenly become anything but routine.

It got my full attention. *It* meant one of my kids was hurt! *It* meant I was needed.

As I rushed back into the house, I saw one-year old Sarah sitting on the living room floor, looking slightly bewildered by all the noise and confusion around her. It was obvious, she was fine. The process of elimination kicked in.

It's not Sarah, so it must be Joe, I concluded instantaneously. But, where is he and what's his problem?

As I ran from the living room, continuing my search, I was met by Susan as she sprinted from one of the back bedrooms. Apparently, she had heard *it*, too. And by the expression on her face, it was clear that she, too, recognized what *it* meant.

We didn't speak. There was no time. We just kept moving.

Together, Susan and I ran through the dining room before making a hard right turn into the kitchen in search of our little boy. And it was there we found him. Standing, dazed and frightened, tears streamed from his eyes as blood streamed from his chin. It was an uncomfortable sight. Joe *was* hurt.

As I bent down and scooped my son up and into my arms, a jagged gash just under his chin became clearly visible. Through the blood I could tell it was a deep cut. In fact, the cut reached all the way to the chin bone. Through a torrent of tears and hardly able to speak beyond his own gasps and sobs, Joe began trying to explain to us what had happened. The message he attempted to communicate came in bursts of incomplete, barely decipherable words and phrases. Nevertheless, I heard things like...

"Climb drawers...want picture...I fall...floor...my chin hurts...I sorry, Daddy...I love you, Mommy."

Listening to Joe's sketchy, incomplete explanation, while surveying the scene around us, Susan and I were soon able to piece together the following.

As soon as Joe saw me leave, though he knew it was wrong to do so, he ran into the kitchen, pulled out the cabinet drawers, then climbed from one drawer to the next to the next, using them as a makeshift ladder. From the top drawer he stepped onto the kitchen counter top. Once on the counter top he balanced precariously—oblivious to the possible danger—stretching and reaching for a picture he wanted that was hanging nearby on the kitchen wall. It was then that lost his balance and fell. In the fall, his chin must have violently struck the ceramic tile floor below. The blow resulted in what I loosely refer to as a "split chin" or "gapper," otherwise interpreted as a cut serious enough that a common band-aid simply wouldn't suffice.

3

As young parents, this was a first for Susan and me. We had never faced a situation quite like this one involving one of our children. Still, neither of us was inclined to melt under the pressure at the first sign of a crisis. Our personalities and emotions weren't wired that way. Therefore, we simply went about the business of recognizing this situation for what it was—an unfortunate accident that needed our immediate attention. This was far from the end of the world and we felt it important that we help Joe, even at his tender age, or more importantly, *because* of his tender age, realize that.

As Susan removed Joe's bloodied shirt, I applied direct pressure to the wound using a damp cloth. With pressure continuing to be applied, Susan proceeded to wash the drying blood off Joe's neck, chest, arms and hands. All the while, we talked calmly to him. In a few short minutes, we had stemmed the flow of both tears and blood. I placed a couple of temporary band-aids over the cut as Susan pulled a clean t-shirt on over his head.

At that point, Joe seemed to take a quick personal inventory of his situation. He could see neither the wound nor its bloody remnants. His blood-stained shirt was no where to be found. His parents seemed to be acting as if everything was normal. From Joe's limited perspective it all added up to one logical conclusion—HE WAS HEALED!

Of course, Susan and I knew better. We knew this ordeal was far from over. There was no sense pretending otherwise. In fact, the most unpleasant part still lay ahead. Joe needed stitches. And to make matters worse, these would be his first! However, the gaping wound, represented by his split chin couldn't be ignored. It had to be repaired.

But Joe didn't know about the inevitable stitches—at least not yet. Should we tell him? we wondered. *Would he understand? If we did tell him, wouldn't that just frighten him unnecessarily? If he knew what was going to happen, wouldn't that make the process even more difficult for the doctor? Joe is much too young to comprehend all this, isn't he?*

Of course, he's too young, I quickly convinced myself. *We'll just wait and deal with all the unpleasantness that accompanies stitches when we can avoid it no longer—at the doctor's office.*

"Joe," I said as calmly as I could, "let's go for a ride. We'll let the doctor take a look at your chin and tell us what he thinks."

Cat Whiskers

Once Sarah was delivered next door to the babysitter, Joe, Susan and I climbed into the minivan for the short ride to the local pediatrician's office. The more I thought about what was to come, the greater the sense of dread that enveloped me. This was one nightmare any parent would have preferred to avoid. But now, that wasn't an option.

As we entered the doctor's office waiting room, I realized just how uncomfortable and inadequate I felt. Susan was the one who usually handled duties such as the kid's medical checkups. She was the one that was more familiar with this place. But this was a job for both of us and I was not about to shirk my responsibility. Once inside, I encouraged Susan and Joe to take a seat near the door, well out of earshot from my planned conversation with the receptionist. They obliged and I walked slowly forward and approached the receptionist's desk alone.

"Um, excuse me," I began haltingly.

"Good morning, sir. How can I help you?" The receptionist's perkiness was in stark contrast to my current dismal state of mind.

"Yeah, um, my name is Phillip Van Hooser. That's my wife and son sitting over there," I said, motioning over my shoulder at the woman with the little boy wiggling in her lap. "His name's Joe. Well, you see, Joe fell and cut his chin a little while ago," I said slowly before leaning slightly closer and whispering, "and he needs stitches."

"Mr. Van Hooser, I certainly understand," she responded knowingly. "I need to tell you though that the doctor on call today is still making his hospital rounds. However, I expect him back in the office within the next half hour or so. Why don't you, your wife and son wait in the examination room? You'll be more comfortable there and as soon as the doctor arrives I'll send him right in. Is that okay?"

"Sure. That sounds fine," I muttered with little enthusiasm.

With that, the young woman directed the three of us to a room down the hall outfitted with the normal doctor "things," an examination table, two chairs and a floor full of toys that any little boy was sure to love. As soon as we entered the room, Joe got excited. Spotting the toys, he immediately threw himself into his play with the exuberance and intensity that only a three-year old can muster—his earlier accident now little more than a distant memory.

Susan and I, on the other hand, were not nearly as excited to be there. While Joe played, we pulled the chairs close by one another and sat, speaking very little, but later realizing that we had been thinking the same basic thought—*Why was it again that we thought we needed children?* Okay, I admit it was no more than a fleeting thought. But, I suspect we weren't the first parents in recorded history to have entertained such a thought briefly at one time or another under similar circumstances.

We settled in and waited.

After about thirty minutes, the door of the examination room suddenly swung open. In walked the person for whom we had been waiting. Though admittedly a stranger to us all, it was obvious he was the doctor. How could I tell? He was the only person in the room wearing a white lab coat, with a stethoscope draped casually around his neck.

As he entered the room, my wife and I stood to introduce ourselves.

"Good morning, Doctor. I'm Phillip Van Hooser," I said, extending my hand to him. "This is my wife, Susan. And over there, that's our son, Joe."

When I had last noticed, just before the doctor entered, Joe had been playing contentedly in the floor on the opposite side of the room. When the door opened and the doctor stepped in, my attention momentarily turned away from Joe and to the doctor. But, now as I looked back to present Joe to the doctor, I realized Joe was no longer playing contentedly in the floor. No, now I noticed that he was on his feet, staring intently upward, directly into the face of this stranger.

The doctor's eyes quickly met Joe's.

"Hi there, Joe," the doctor offered warmly.

With absolutely no hesitation, Joe crossed his little arms, stared defiantly at the doctor and declared forcefully, "I ain't gettin' no stitches!"

My son's proper use of the English language left much to be desired. But the clarity and resolve with which he delivered his singular message was nothing short of impressive. And frankly, it caught me off guard.

I admit hearing Joe speak up so quickly and directly was somewhat less shocking than the unexpected message his words conveyed. You see, I was absolutely certain that neither Susan nor I had mentioned the subject of stitches to Joe. In fact, we had intentionally avoided the subject. However, it was now clear that Joe had some hidden reservoir of information, some sort of intuitive sense that until now had been unknown to us. In other words, our son knew more than he was letting on. And our son, our three-year old son, apparently had a mind of his own. And he wasn't afraid to speak that mind. Imagine that!

I pause here, wondering how many other times in our lives we intentionally tip-toe around sensitive issues, thinking that in doing so we are actually protecting some person from the harsh reality of the situation. When, in reality, that person is already well aware of the situation—be it good or bad, pleasant or undesirable.

Hearing clearly the words that Joe had spoken, I stole a quick glance at the good doctor. By all outward indications he appeared unshaken by Joe's sharp retort. In fact, he spoke up quickly in response.

"Well, do you mind if I have a look at your chin anyway, Joe?" he asked.

Joe agreed to this simple request and the doctor leaned forward, gently removing the band-aids covering the cut. Once uncovered, the doctor surveyed the chin quickly before straightening back up. Now the doctor began shaking his head slightly back and forth, while stroking his own chin thoughtfully. All the while Joe eyed him with suspicious curiosity. After several more seconds of silence, the doctor addressed Joe once again.

"Well, Joe, it looks like you've got a real problem," the doctor finally said in a very matter-of-fact manner.

"What is it?" Joe asked curiously.

"Well, you said you didn't want stitches. But, from what I can tell by looking at your chin, if we don't sew it up, the next time you start eating a pork chop, it might slip through that hole and fall out onto your lap."

Joe's expression, in response to this thought, was priceless. His eyes got bigger, his head jerked back slightly and an innocent grin creased his lips. Joe wasn't expecting such a fun, casual response—and frankly, neither were we. Nevertheless, this non-serious comment worked its magic. It was immediately obvious that this doctor had succeeded in capturing our son's attention and imagination, and possibly, his respect as well.

The doctor continued.

"Joe, we need to talk."

With those simple words, the doctor knelt down, picked my son up and sat him on the edge of the examination table. Once Joe was seated, the doctor bent down and leaned in close. His face and eyes mere inches from Joe's. Though Susan and I stood nearby, Joe seemed oblivious to our presence, focused instead on this interesting doctor. It was then that the doctor started talking in earnest with his patient.

"Joe, I've been thinking. Your chin needs to be sewn up. But, you said you didn't want stitches. So, I tell you what I'm going to do. I'm not going to give you stitches. No, sir, you're special. And because you're special, I'm going to give you 'cat whiskers.'"

Cat whiskers? Cat whiskers! Hmmm, that sounds interesting, Joe must have been thinking. But, whether that's what Joe thought or not, there is one thing that was certain—this doctor knew how to hold a three-year old's attention. He was a pro. And I was beginning to realize that the chances were pretty good that he had done this sort of thing before.

As Joe continued to consider the concept of "cat whiskers," the doctor spoke up again.

"But, before I give you those cat whiskers, it's very important that you know *how* it's all going to happen."

With that simple statement and with no further warning, the doctor reached into the pocket of his lab coat and produced the object that I had dreaded. It was a syringe. Exactly the same type of syringe that another doctor had waved in front of my face sixteen years earlier following one of my high school football games. You see, I had been injured—a split chin—during the game. Yet, all these many years later I still remembered the play during which I was hurt. I remembered the blood. And I remembered the needle. Oh, how I remembered the needle! And I remembered how it felt as the point of that needle entered the open wound in my chin and the searing pain surged from the split in my chin to the soles of my feet. These long suppressed memories surfaced quickly as I watched this well-meaning doctor holding his syringe in the air for Joe to see.

NO, NO, NO! I thought to myself momentarily. *Don't SHOW him the needle! SNEAK UP ON HIM!*

But this doctor had other ideas. And as I was to soon discover—his ideas were better.

"Joe, do you know what this is?" he asked, holding the syringe so Joe could see it clearly.

Joe nodded. "It's a needle."

"That's right. Now, do you know what I'm going to do with this needle?"

"Not yet," Joe responded guardedly.

"Well, Joe, before I can give you those cat whiskers, I'm going to have to give you a shot with a needle like this in your chin. To be honest, I'll have to give you at least two shots, maybe even three. And Joe, I need to tell you, these shots are going to hurt—but they won't hurt very long."

"How long?" Joe asked.

"What do you mean?"

"How long will it hurt?"

"Oh, well, now that's a good question," the doctor responded. "Let's see. Can you count to ten?"

"Yes, sir," Joe said with an obvious sense of personal pride.

"Well, Joe, by the time you count to ten, the shots will be over and it will quit hurting. After that, while I'm giving you the cat whiskers, all you'll feel are little tugs. Just like this." (The doctor demonstrated with a little pinch and slight tug on Joe's chin.) "See that won't hurt a bit. Do you understand what I'm telling you, Joe?"

Joe listened carefully, apparently working to process both the good and bad of all that he was hearing.

"I think so."

"Well, then, Joe, there's only one other problem we have to attend to."

"What is it?" Joe asked innocently.

"Well, it wouldn't even be a problem if you were a *big* boy. *Big* boys could do this job easily. But, I don't know about you, Joe. You're still such a *little* boy. And this job is for a *big* boy. I don't think a *little* boy would even want to tackle it. Yeah, if only you were a *big* boy..."

The doctor went on and on, being intentionally elusive about the specific job to be done, while over-emphasizing the important contrast between *little* boys and *big* boys.

It didn't take Joe long to get a belly full of that. Joe was three years old and like most of his three year old male counterparts, he was sick and tired of hearing all that *little* boy stuff.

"*I'm* a *big* boy!" Joe finally declared emphatically.

"You are? Well, that's great news!" the doctor exclaimed. "I was afraid you weren't big enough to do this job. But you said you're a big boy and I believe you are. So, Joe, here's what I need you to do. I need for you to lie down on this table, put your hands under your butt, stick your chin way up in the air so I can shine this big light on it and finally, I need for you to lie really still until I get you fixed up with these cat whiskers. Joe, do you really think you're big enough to do all that?"

"Yes, sir!"

"Great. Let's get started then."

As an eyewitness to the entire event, with absolutely no more encouragement than that just mentioned, I watched as our three year old voluntarily laid down on the table, shoved his hands under his rear end, stuck his chin high in the air and froze as stiff as if he were a statue.

At about that same time, the door to the examination room opened and in walked two nurses. I'd been expecting the "restraining crew." Nevertheless, I couldn't bear the thought of Joe being physically man-handled or worse still, strapped into a restraining device by strangers. For that reason, I had already intentionally positioned myself on the opposite side of the table from the where the doctor would be working. Though I didn't look forward to the experience, I felt that if my son needed to be restrained in order for the doctor to do his work, it ought to be his father, not some stranger.

But, initially at least, such concerns proved to be unwarranted. One of the two nurses did walk to the table. Once there, she positioned herself directly behind Joe's head, gently reaching up and placing her hands along each side of his temples. Now, let's be clear. Her job was not to restrain this little boy. There is no reasonable way she—or anyone else for that matter—could have restrained an excited three-year old, intent on resisting, had she wanted to. No, she wasn't there to restrain him. Primarily, she was there to reassure him.

Meanwhile, nurse number two took up a position near the door, standing quietly, calling no undue attention to herself.

All the while, the doctor went about his business of preparing needles and cat whiskers, while still engaging his young patient in good natured conversation. Eventually, all was made ready. The doctor approached the boy on the table.

"Joe, are you ready to get started?" he asked.

"Yes, sir," was Joe's steady reply.

"Okay then..."

As the doctor, needle in hand, approached Joe's chin, my heart sank. At that moment I would have gladly volunteered to take a dozen shots in place of my son. But, that's not the way life works. Difficulties are no respecter of age. Difficulties find us all. And all of us must learn to face the difficulties we encounter in our own way.

At the very instant that the cold steel of the needle pierced the open flesh of Joe's chin; as those nerve endings came alive; as the involuntary electrical impulses raced through the central nervous system on their way to this little boy's brain; as the brain collected the barrage of incoming information, instantaneously processing this information and ultimately determining that a pain reaction was justified...as all of this happened, Joe uttered an involuntary guttural moan.

"Unngh!" he said.

Here we go, I thought as I braced myself for the untold unpleasantness that was sure to follow.

Then this single utterance acknowledging the pain Joe was feeling was followed shortly thereafter by...nothing. That's right, nothing. No screaming. No crying. No fighting. No thrashing about in an attempt to escape. No movement of any kind. In fact, Joe never even took his hands out from under his little butt. He simply said, "Unngh!"

But Joe's response triggered a counter-response by the doctor. The doctor began talking calmly, or to be more accurate, he began counting calmly.

"One...two...three...," he counted slowly and out loud so Joe could hear him, as he continued to methodically inject the pain deadening concoction. "Four...five...six..."

When the doctor spoke the word "six," Joe could hold back no longer.

"SEVEN, EIGHT, NINE, TEN!" Joe said loudly and more quickly, emphasizing by the pace and tone of his words his impatience with the doctor's slower-than-desired counting rhythm. *If the period of the pain is directly related to counting to ten like the doctor told me, then let's count faster!* Joe seemed to be reasoning.

It was a light moment that arrived just when the tension was highest. Joe's unexpected response drew immediate chuckles from all of us gathered there in the room. Though his response was unplanned, even Joe seemed to appreciate that the least little bit of laughter could help the medicine go down (or in) a little easier.

For the next fifteen minutes or so, Joe proved more than worthy of "big boy" status and acknowledgement. During his entire time on the table, Joe continued to lie ramrod straight, hands securely beneath him, with his chin jutted forward as requested by the doctor. After the injections had been completed and the numbing effects of the medication had kicked in, the doctor proceeded to repair the wound with a grand total of five stitches, er, excuse me—cat whiskers. Throughout the surgical procedure Joe engaged in friendly, light-hearted banter with the doctor and nurse—and all this without the least little bit of physical restraint. From my perspective, the scene that I witnessed was nothing short of amazing.

When the doctor finally announced that the repairs were complete, Joe popped up on the table, looked at him once more and offered a polite, "Thank you, sir."

YEESSS! That's my boy. Obviously, a chip off the old block! Were a few of the admittedly proud, even self-serving thoughts that raced through my mind in that moment of wonder and triumph.

The Power of Dairy Queen and Toys 'R Us

I admit to being absolutely astounded by what I had been privileged to witness! It was obvious that Joe had performed magnificently—far beyond anything I could have hoped or imagined. My cup of fatherly pride was filled to overflowing as I watched and considered the way my young son had conducted himself throughout this unpleasant ordeal.

But I must admit I was also confused. Confused by things that had turned out very differently than I would have predicted at the beginning of this "adventure." Joe had behaved in ways that I simply had not expected. Why was that? What made that happen?

Suddenly, an old leadership lesson came to mind. It was a simple lesson I had learned as a young corporate manager many years prior and one that I had since shared with many of the leaders I had been privileged to train, coach and counsel:

Positive personal performance should always be recognized and re-warded in a public way in hopes that such performance will be repeated in private.

That's exactly what I need to do, I thought. *I need to recognize and reward Joe's positive behavior here today, in hopes that he will remember and repeat such behavior in the future.*

I swept Joe into my arms and lifted him off the table. Susan and I both smothered him with hugs, kisses and positive reinforcement. On our way out of the office, I thanked the doctor and the nurse for their help, before turning my attention once again to Joe.

Now what can I do to reward Joe's behavior that will make him want to do it again? I wondered as we drove from the doctor's office back home. *I know. I'll take him to Dairy Queen for ice cream and then we will make a trip to Toys 'R Us for some sort of special toy.*

I shared these thoughts with Joe, to his obvious delight. I promised him that later that day, when both of these businesses opened, we would visit them together. It was the least I could do for the hero of the hour—my son, Joe.

Soon the three of us were home again. Once there, Susan quickly decided her time would be better spent on this day at home with her kids, instead of in the office with me. She was convinced that Joe needed an extra helping of TLC and she was the perfect one to provide it. Joe and Sarah were thrilled to have mom all to themselves.

Conversely, I couldn't wait to get to the office. I had an unexpected task that had been dropped into my lap. Now it was time to wrestle with it. The task before me needed some focused, uninterrupted thought. While this whole unbelievable experience was still fresh in my mind, I needed to sit down and figure out exactly why Joe had performed so heroically.

Everyone Needs A Hero

Upon arriving at my office, I sat quietly at my desk for a long while pondering the unexpected events of the morning. The experience I had witnessed was simply impossible for me to ignore or casually set aside. There had been too much mental, sensory and emotional stimulation to simply walk away and discount the entire chain of events as being somehow normal or unworthy of further consideration. Something special had happened in that doctor's office. I was certain of it. I was there. But, I was also perplexed. What was it? What had gotten into Joe to make him act as he had?

In an attempt to capture and somehow organize the random thoughts and images that were banging around in my head—thoughts of bloody t-shirts, tears, toys, needles, cat whiskers and unexpected courage—I reached for a pad of notebook paper. For the next several minutes I worked diligently, trying to reconstruct in some sort of sequential, linear fashion, the events that had unfolded that morning. But try as I might, the effort proved most frustrating. My mind wasn't interested in linear thinking. Mentally, I kept leap-frogging forward to the images of that brave little boy in that doctor's office examination room and the extraordinary behavior I witnessed while he was on that table.

Suddenly, a singular and admittedly, very pleasing thought registered in my brain.

Kids fall and hurt themselves every day. There's nothing particularly special about that. But most kids simply wouldn't have responded with the self-control and self-restraint that my son did. Heck, that makes Joe a hero!

Ordaining Heroes

Spurred on by this sudden burst of inspiration, I flipped to a clean page of paper and hastily, I wrote in big, bold letters two words across the top of the page:

JOE — HERO

Honestly, that's how I was feeling at that moment—my young son was my hero. But, was it all adrenaline and emotion or was there really something important that I could learn from this experience? For the past fifteen years I had been methodically evaluating virtually every positive experience—personal or professional—for the lessons it might yield. I was constantly on the lookout for high performing individuals (even if they were only three years old and related to me). I wanted to know what they did that made them so successful. But, even more importantly, I wanted to know why they did what they did—and how those lessons might work for others.

On the surface, the task seemed easy enough. I figured I would spend a few minutes jotting down the specific things I had witnessed Joe do—the things that made him obviously so special—and the rest would become crystal clear. And that's exactly what I tried to do.

But I soon discovered the task was far from easy. Oh, there were a number of specific things I had witnessed Joe do that were worthy of note. But upon closer examination of each, I had to admit that Joe's behavior, as positive and encouraging as it was, was simply a reaction to some other sort of stimulation. In other words, Joe's ultimate behavior—as positive and heroic as it proved to be—was, in large part, a the result of his personal choice to follow the lead of someone else.

After several agonizingly, futile minutes of trying to create the "hero son" I wanted so desperately, I came to an eye-opening realization. As remarkably as Joe had performed under difficult circumstances in the doctor's office, Joe was *not* the hero of this story. He was not personally responsible for creating and managing the environment that fostered such remarkable and unexpected behavior. That distinction belonged to the doctor in charge. I began to realize that the doctor was the one who had focused like a laser on his patient's problems, rather than on the problems the patient might cause. He was the one who created an environment in which positive communication ruled. He seemed to confidently expect the best outcome and then consciously chose to communicate in such a way as to assure the best outcome.

Eventually, it became clear to me that there certainly *was* a hero in this story—it just happened to be the doctor.

I flipped to a second page of the notebook and wrote in big, bold letters:

DOCTOR—HERO

I then began to carefully reconsider what this special doctor, this master communicator, had done while working his medical magic with my son. It didn't take long to realize no hocus-pocus was involved. Instead, this doctor employed a focused communication method that yielded the type of results that could easily be mistaken for magic.

Putting the Magic to Work

In less than ten minutes, I was able to identify a six communication principles – eighteen magical words – six principles with the power and potential to change the way anyone communicates—for the better—forever!

What were these principles?

Principle #1: Talk With People

Principle #2: Explain the Process

Principle #3: Tell the Truth

Principle #4: Work for Understanding

Principle #5: Get Others Involved

Principle #6: Do Your Job

These six critical principles are analyzed in the following six chapters. But, recognizing these six critical principles was just the first step in redefining my approach to inspired interpersonal communication. As I began to consider and analyze these principles more thoroughly, the prize came clearly into view—communicating with power and effectiveness forever!

Principle #1

Talk With People

Most of us readily agree with the importance of great communication skills in building solid, long term personal and professional relationships. And on the surface, the act of person-to-person communication seems simple enough. After all, we've been involved in the process of learning to communicate since we were babes in our mother's arms. One would assume that after twenty, thirty, forty or even fifty years of practice, we should expect a higher level of communication expertise than is normally displayed in our daily interpersonal encounters. But, in life, reality often trumps assumptions. If outward appearances are at all a reliable yardstick, we must accept the fact that a majority of people we encounter in our daily routines simply can't communicate well—or worse still, they won't.

In revisiting the specific actions of Joe's doctor, my thoughts revert to the first impression the doctor made as he entered that examination room. At the time, the act seemed so insignificant, so relatively unimportant that I almost missed it. But, had I missed it, I would have missed the very foundation on which this remarkable encounter was to be built. By recognizing it, I came to realize that what the doctor did was not only foundational—it was intentional. The doctor knew exactly what he was doing and why he was doing it. Like any good communicator, he was setting the stage for the positive communication environment and the anticipated results that would follow.

What exactly did this doctor do that was so special? Upon entering the room, from the very first moment, this enlightened physician engaged in a focused effort to connect with people, in particular, his young patient. This doctor was on a mission. It was not just a mission of mercy and healing. It began as a mission of connecting and hearing. The doctor knew that for him to be successful in the work he was to do, he must first win the trust and acceptance of the person with whom he would be working.

The Value of First Impressions

All of us can remember occasions early in life where we were coached, even cajoled, by parents, grandparents, teachers, and other adult authority figures about the value and importance of "first impressions." I remember being reminded time and again, "Phil, you only have one opportunity to make a good first impression." It was true then and it continues to be true today. However, in the midst of our fast paced lives these days it seems that far too many of us have forgotten, discounted or ignored completely the foundational importance of making good first impressions in our communications.

You already know that the good doctor did a commendable job of greeting my wife and me, before focusing his laser-like attention on Joe. In the moments that followed, the doctor didn't talk with me about Joe—he turned to Joe and said, "Come here, Joe. We need to talk." The doctor proceeded to talk directly with Joe—while allowing my wife and I to listen. It may sound easy enough to do, but in reality, *talking with*, instead of *to*, individuals can be a very difficult task.

Consider for a moment what might have occurred had things started differently that morning. What if the doctor had simply chosen to disregard the importance of positive connection and first impressions and instead, had focused solely on the technical task at hand—sewing up Joe's split chin. After all that was what we there for, wasn't it?

Assume that such a focused, albeit non-communicative doctor had entered the room with a nurse or assistant in tow. While barking orders over his shoulder, he might have felt compelled to offer an obligatory glance, nod and grunt in the general direction of the patient and his parents. But that's probably about all. This was a busy man and he wanted all in his wake to know it. He had no time for warm, fuzzy personal greetings or other frivolous pleasantries.

There was physical healing to be done and other patients to be attended to. This doctor was all business.

"The child weighs thirty-six pounds? Okay, prepare four CCs of Novacaine and secure a supply of 3.0 silk. Also, retrieve the Papoose Board and prepare the patient for confined immobilized restriction."

Such words and actions might reinforce this doctor's scientific medical proficiency. However, what about the patient? Isn't he an active partner in this process? From the moment this physician entered the room, his people skills and so called "bedside manner" were on display for all to see—for good or for bad. By the time the doctor has chosen to finally turn and involve the patient, the opportunity for a personal connection to be made has long since passed. The doctor has taken no substantive steps toward earning the patient's trust. As a result, the encounter has a greater possibility of being more confrontational than consultative with more communication problems to follow.

A Friendly Face in an Unlikely Place

Most of us live busy lives. Busy lives can be good. Busy lives can produce a myriad of personal experiences, professional accomplishments, even diverse and valued relationships. But there is a fine line between being *busy* and being *too busy*. When we find ourselves being *too busy*, it is possible that we will thoughtlessly and unintentionally ignore the more important things—and people—that add true value and worth to our lives.

Often, when we find ourselves being *too busy*, that's the exact time that we need to talk. We need to talk to people about the things we notice, feel, appreciate and value.

Several years ago, I found myself in a southwestern city where I was scheduled to give a morning leadership presentation. I arrived early for the session which was to be held in the local municipal convention center. I was so early the entire facility appeared to me to be deserted.

After locating and familiarizing myself with the room in which I would be speaking, I took the opportunity to make a quick trip to the men's room. As I found the restroom and stepped through the door, I was stopped in my tracks by the smell. It could not be ignored. But it was not the type of smell that many of us have come to expect when entering public restrooms. No, this was a pleasing aroma rather than a foul odor. I would actually describe it as being remarkably "fresh and clean."

I would soon realize that the welcoming aroma was but one positive indicator of other good things to come. For example, the restroom's entry way corridor was absolutely spotless! Now, don't misunderstand. It was by no means adorned with expensive marble or tile, the type of wall and floor coverings favored by the world's finest hotels. No, this was a public facility, undoubtedly financed with taxpayer dollars. Its construction materials were concrete blocks covered with enamel paint. Nevertheless, the sinks, counter tops, urinals, toilets, floors and walls, basic as they were, were so clean it was impossible not to notice.

I paused momentarily to admire this unexpected phenomenon. Suddenly I sensed something—or someone—behind me. Startled, I whirled around and came face-to-face with a middle aged man, coming around the corner, holding a mop. Admittedly, his presence caught me off guard. Before I really had time to think about what to say or how I might best say it, I found myself blurting out these words, "Are you responsible for cleaning this restroom?"

As soon as the words had exited my mouth, I realized that I had emphasized the word *you* just a bit too aggressively, as in, "Are YOU responsible for cleaning this restroom?" And given this gentleman's immediate reaction, I realized my words and their delivery had, unfortunately, been misinterpreted. I instantly sensed that the first impression I had created was far from what I had intended. My words had been delivered in haste, brought on by this stranger's unexpected appearance. As a result, even I could hear the unintended accusatory tone that engulfed my question.

The man paused and slowly raised his head. He leaned forward slightly on the mop handle. He looked at me suspiciously.

"Yeah, why?" he responded curtly, with an obvious note of defensiveness in his voice.

Realizing that my opportunity to make a positive first impression was rapidly evaporating, I chose honesty as my method of recovery.

"Well, I really didn't know anyone was in here. I thought I was all alone. And to be honest, you startled me. But when I saw you holding that mop, I figured you were responsible. I just want you to know how much I appreciate this clean restroom."

The man stared at me in silence for a few seconds, obviously considering my words, all the while trying to determine my level of sincerity. Finally, he broke the silence with a question of his own.

"For real?" he asked simply.

"For real," I responded. "Listen, my job causes me to travel several days each week all over the country. As a result, I end up using other people's restrooms more than I do my own. Too often, the public restrooms I encounter are simply disgusting. But as soon as I walked in the door here, I couldn't help but notice what a great job you have done with this restroom. I just wanted you to know that I appreciate it and I appreciate you for making the effort to do what is necessary to keep it in such excellent condition."

The man whose shirt bore the name "Henry," over his heart, looked long and hard at me, as he continued to consider the words I had just spoken. I felt certain he was trying to determine for himself whether I had been truly genuine in the comments I had just offered or if I had some hidden ulterior motive. Finally convinced of my earnestness, this restroom attendant spoke up once more. His words have stayed with me till this day.

Looking directly into my eyes, he said, "Thanks, buddy. I really appreciate that you noticed my work." Then he added wistfully, "Nobody has ever told me that before."

My conversation with Henry was brief. And it began rather auspiciously. Nevertheless, in a matter of seconds, in the most unlikely of places, Henry and I connected and talked with one another. In so doing, a rudimentary, beginning level of trust was established between us. Obviously, this one-on-one communication was of a different variety than that which transpired between the doctor and my son. However, it was no less important in building trust, a positive first impression and a foundation on which future communication and interaction could conceivably be constructed.

Communication's Magnetic Appeal

Let's face it, good communicators are like magnets. They draw people to themselves.

Like it or not, we are all measured to one degree or another by our ability to communicate. And the more successful we are as individual communicators, the more successful we can become in every aspect of our lives. Whether athlete or academic, banker or baker, politician or policewoman—everyone can benefit personally and professionally by enhancing their ability to communicate successfully, nose-to-nose and toes-to-toes, with others.

So, a couple of logical questions naturally follow, "How can I attract people with my ability to communicate? How can I successfully learn to *talk with people*?

Here are some ideas to consider.

When Talking With People...
Earn Their Trust by Taking Responsibility

The foundation of any trust relationship is the belief that the person I am choosing to trust is ready and willing to take responsibility for his actions. In the context of interpersonal communication, the person who initiates the communication must readily accept the responsibility for making the communication effort successful. If communication fails, the person who initiated the communication should never say, "It was his fault or her fault." The initiator of the communication must be willing to shoulder the blame for the failed communication.

It is true that no one person can control every aspect of multi-person communication. However, in too many instances the persons who undertake the communication activity, when they encounter obstacles, just quit trying. They give up. They abandon the cause. Great communicators simply can't afford to do that. If our communication efforts are floundering, we must step back and fashion some different communication approach. Failure is not an option. Successful communicators are creative and inventive enough to find a way to succeed. The doctor took responsibility for establishing trust and rapport with his young patient. Not knowing whether it would work or not, he simply took responsibility for making positive, interactive communication happen, in a non-traditional way—and it worked. We must be willing and committed to doing the same.

When Talking With People...Show Genuine Concern

Genuine concern can't be faked. In one-on-one communication, if one party senses the other playing some sort of game or is somehow attempting to manipulate the process for his or her own benefit, healthy communication is certain to falter. It falters because the foundation of trust and connection, if it was ever there to begin with, begins to erode and crumble. The communication environment shifts from being one in which I can trust the motives of my communication partner, to one in which it becomes a dog-eat-dog, every-man-for-himself activity.

Genuine concern is never a byproduct of casually talking about, talking around, talking behind, talking over or talking down to someone else. Genuine concern can only be fostered by *talking with* an individual and thereby learning more about his unique circumstance—his needs, wants, desires, hopes, dreams, fears, failures, anxieties, and so on. From this position of understanding comes the empathy necessary to be of assistance to others. Empathy is not to be confused with sympathy. Sympathy is feeling sorry for something or someone. Empathy is *feeling as they feel*. When you learn to feel as others feel, you have overcome one of the significant barriers to communication that some individuals never recognize.

The doctor knew Joe didn't want—was actually fearful of receiving—stitches. Because of the empathetic approach the doctor chose, he found a way to redirect the young boy's fear of stitches to his curiosity with "cat whiskers." True concern for others serves to tap into our reservoir of ingenuity in an effort to connect more successfully with them.

When Talking With People…Learn to Listen, but Listen to Learn

Let's be honest, listening is a formidable task which far too few have mastered. I often ask my audiences how many of them consider themselves to be good listeners. I rarely get more than five percent of the audience to claim strong listening skills. Yet, when I ask how many people have dedicated themselves to becoming better listeners still almost no hands are raised. I am left to wonder, if we know we are not great listeners, why aren't we taking aggressive steps forward to remedy that situation?

Listening is not a spectator sport. Good listening—and what one will learn from the activity—requires focused attention and continual engagement. Without the will and ability to listen actively, one will never truly be able to *talk with people*. To talk with people, you must be able to listen to what they are saying, discern their intent and counter with some sort of customized response which dovetails with what you have already heard and learned from the other person. In turn, the other person will continue to share more and more information because they are impressed with your ability and willingness to listen to them.

Here are a few simple tips that can improve your listening habits almost immediately:

- *Look directly at the other person while he or she is speaking.*

- *Don't fidget or play with objects that can be distracting.*

- *Ask questions to clarify what is being said.*

- *Show concern by fashioning some questions that deal with the person's feelings.*

- *Don't interrupt unnecessarily; be patient and attentive.*

- *Don't change the subject until all parties are ready to do so.*

- *Remain poised and emotionally controlled.*

- *Repeat some of the things that are said to give indication of connectedness.*

Principle # 2

Explain the Process

"I didn't actually tell her, but I'm sure she knows what I mean."

How many times have you heard such a statement? More importantly, how many times have you said or thought the same? Unless the person you're thinking of is a certified mind reader (I've never met one of those), choosing to believe that any person will know what you are thinking without making the effort to tell them is the equivalent of actually believing you will win the lottery. It *could* happen—unfortunately, it seldom does.

Let's be clear. Assumptions are a fool's folly and the obvious mark of a lazy communicator. "To assume" something provides evidence that one is too lazy to ask, share, verify and evaluate. Besides being seen as lazy, people who deal in unverified assumptions leave themselves open to a myriad of communication disconnects and breakdowns. It's never a question *if* making assumptions will get you into trouble. The real questions are: When will the troubles begin? Where might they crop up? With whom will I have problems? And how much will my errant assumptions actually cost me in time, dollars and goodwill?

Joe's doctor, this story's communication hero, did what all of us have the capacity to do. The doctor had the good sense to take the time up front to *explain the process* to the one who was about to be impacted. Simple as that. He didn't assume that he knew all about Joe's fears and anxieties—he asked. He didn't assume that Joe knew how his wound would be repaired—he shared. He didn't assume that Joe would know which instruments would be used and for what purposes—he verified. He didn't assume anything. To the contrary, he evaluated and explained everything.

We should never assume that others know what we are up to, even those closest to us. We may think that choosing to avoid these "unnecessary" explanations up front will save us time in the process. What we don't consider is that sooner or later we are sure to end up explaining the process anyway—what we did, how it was done and why we did it. If the process is explained *before* action is taken, most people are still open to listening and learning. However, if explanations are offered *after* action has been taken, many people will already be dealing with the frustration brought on by what they see as your insufficient communication approach.

We learned way back in preschool that "a stitch in time saves nine." It's true. And it's also true that a little communication planning can make the difference between a motivated individual committed to excellence and someone who is confused, frustrated and looking to do just enough to get by.

Look Busy

I was sixteen years old and had been hired for my first "real" job. I had grown up working on the family farm. But this was the first job for which I would go off to work each day with scheduled hours, established responsibilities, benefits (as minimal as they were) and a fixed roof over my head. I saw this as a great opportunity. Working in a feed mill—a place that supplied hog and cattle feed to farmers—might not be your idea of a dream job. But I saw it differently. I saw this job as an entry level position in the agricultural industry. I expected to learn new skills, prove my worth and begin my journey toward professional independence. I was excited by the possibilities.

I arrived at work that first day a good twenty minutes prior to my scheduled start time. I was bound and determined to make a good first impression. The personnel representative had advised me to report to the shop building on the first morning and that I would meet my supervisor there. He hadn't bothered to share the supervisor's name in advance and I had been hesitant to ask.

With some normal first-day trepidation, I walked into the shop building and stood, looking around. The room was empty except for one person. A middle aged man, sat at a table at the far end of the room with his head bowed over a newspaper spread out on the table before him. He never looked up. He seemed much more intent on his paper and the cup of coffee in his left hand and the cigarette in his right.

I approached the man tentatively.

"Excuse me, my name is Phil. I've been hired to work here this summer. I was told I would meet my supervisor here, but I don't know his name," I admitted rather nervously.

The man slowly looked up at me from beneath the bill of his well worn cap. He looked me over for a few seconds and then shook his head slightly, as if to say "here we go again," before returning his eyes to his paper.

"Earl," he growled lowly.

I was confused. *Does he think my name is Earl?* I didn't know.

"Sir, I'm sorry, but my name is Phil, not Earl."

"I know who *you* are," he growled again, this time more loudly than before. "I'm telling you who your boss is. Earl. Your boss is Earl," he said, before adding, "and that's me. Where's the other boy?"

"I'm sorry, Mr. Earl. Um, I don't know who you're talking about," I responded.

"It's not Mr. Earl—just Earl—I work for a living. They told me I would have two kids to baby sit, er, I mean supervise this summer." Earl chuckled at his own little joke. "You're one of them, now where's the other one?"

"I, um, I don't really know."

My new supervisor, Earl, just shook his head again.

"He probably won't even show. You can't find kids that want to work anymore," he said out loud, but more to himself than to me. He drew a deep breath and then sighed mightily.

"Well, come on," he said as crushed out his cigarette and stood, leaving the paper and coffee cup where they were. I sensed he had plans to return to both shortly.

Earl walked briskly through the swinging doors that opened from the shop into a dark, dusty warehouse beyond. I followed dutifully a few steps behind. We walked past stack after stack of livestock feed staged on pallets lining the exterior wall of the building.

Places like this were already familiar to me—or at least I thought so. Growing up around a farm, I had visited feed mills many times to buy feed for our livestock. But as Earl continued to walk without speaking, I looked around and realized for the first time how very little I knew about businesses like this. But, I was anxious to learn. I wanted to know more. I wanted to do more. My excitement surged again.

Finally, Earl led me to a large feed bin tucked away in a remote corner of the building.

"Boy, I don't have a lot of time," he began, "so pay attention. This is a feed bin. It's full of more than two thousand pounds of feed. Your job is to get the feed out of the bin and into these sacks. Each filled sack should weigh fifty pounds—not forty nine and not fifty one. Fifty pounds exactly. Weigh 'em on those scales there. Got it?"

"Yes, sir," I said, as I hastily made mental notes of what I was being told.

Earl then reached and took an empty sack from a pile lying nearby. He demonstrated how to open the sack, loop the sack's edges over a lip on the bin's emptying chute and then pull the bin's lever to release the bin's contents. He *showed* but he didn't *tell*. There was no explanation of the overall process whatsoever. I had no idea what kind of feed was in the bin. I had no idea as to how many of these bins would be emptied and bagged in a day, week or month. I had no idea if this was the full extent of what I would be doing for the summer or if this was just one of many activities in which I would be involved. I had no idea because Earl chose not to tell me. All I knew was what I was expected to do in that moment.

When Earl had the sack filled with fifty pounds of feed, he pushed it toward me and instructed me to tie the top of the sack tightly with a grass string and then carry it across the building where I was to stack it and the others to follow on designated pallets. Earl told me to continue the routine until I had emptied the bin completely and had packed and stacked all forty plus sacks. It wasn't brain surgery. It was back-breaking physical labor. But, I was young and accustomed to physical labor. What I wasn't used to was such token communication.

"Boy, just keep doing what I've told you until that bin is empty and those sacks of feed are tied and stacked. I should be back before you finish, but if I'm not, just grab a broom and start sweeping. I'll be around before long."

This all happened many years ago. I naturally understand more now than then. Even though I found it strange at the time that there was so little initial conversation and explanation regarding the overall business, the task at hand, the end users of our products and so on, I thought I knew what my primary objective was. At the time, I thought Earl didn't give me much instruction because he saw me as being bright and capable of completing this and other jobs he would assign me.

And because I assumed Earl saw the best in me, I was motivated and absolutely threw myself into my work. I was determined to do an excellent job and by so doing, prove my value and worth to both Earl and the organization.

For the next hour I worked with a vengeance. Every sack had *exactly* fifty pounds. Every sack was tied securely. Every sack was stacked evenly. I worked steadily without taking a break. The sweat rolled. Soon the bin was empty. Earl was nowhere in sight.

I'm working faster than he expected, I thought. Earl will be pleased when he returns and sees how much I have accomplished in so little time.

My self-assured attitude fueled my continued effort. I snatched up a broom and started sweeping. In short order, I had that dusty feed room floor clean enough to eat off. It was then that I paused long enough to take inventory of my recent accomplishments. The bin was empty, the sacks were filled and stacked, the floor was virtually spotless. I had accomplished all that had been assigned me. Satisfied that my efforts would exceed Earl's every expectation, I decided to position myself in the middle of the floor and await his return.

So there I stood, broom in hand, proudly waiting the return of my new supervisor. But, what happened next was not what I would have predicted.

As Earl casually rounded the corner headed for the bin, he looked up and spied me standing in the middle of the floor, broom and all. He stopped abruptly. I watched his head jerk back and forth, left to right as he surveyed the scene around him.

I watched this man with great interest, trying to read his every movement and the mood it represented. Having known Earl for less than an hour, I was not well acquainted with his communication nuances. Still, being the optimist I was, I expected him at any moment to break into a toothy grin and begin repeating over and over, "There is one! There is one young person who still knows how to work. There is one who still cares about the job he does. And I've found him!"

How could Earl not be thrilled with my results? I had done well the job I had been given. That was obvious. Therefore, why wouldn't I expect my positive performance to be rewarded in some way? But my reward was not forthcoming. No effusive praise, no positive affirmations, not even a smile and knowing nod. Since the process had not been explained to me, I was unaware that Earl's reaction was less a result of what he saw and more a result of what he valued. Apparently, Earl valued activity, not accomplishment. I say that because of the question he asked next.

Earl, obviously confused by all that he was witnessing, seemed exasperated. He kept looking around before finally blurting out his central question in a loud, accusatory voice, "WHAT ARE YOU DOING?"

By now, his confusion had confused me. I *thought* what I was doing was rather obvious. I was doing what I had been told to do. And I was doing a good job at it. But rather than say that directly and risk appearing arrogant, I opted for what I thought was a safer answer.

"I'm just standing here," I said meekly.

To which Earl immediately and in an even louder voice responded, "WELL, BOY, DON'T YOU KNOW HOW TO LOOK BUSY?"

Though young and inexperienced, I was a quick study. I began to realize that though unaware of it up until that point, Earl and I had been working from two very different perspectives. Earl embraced his low expectations of young people and their overall work ethic and therefore, simply because I was young, he expected very little in terms of productive output from me. I sensed he was more interested in seeing me do something than seeing what I had done. I, on the other hand, had been taught to do the very best job I could for those who hire me on any job I am assigned. These two divergent thought processes had suddenly collided in front of a bin that dispensed hog feed.

Failure to Communicate

Such unexpected failures to communicate are not at all uncommon. It can happen between any variety of individuals representing different generations and genders, dialects and dispositions. It could even have happened to a pediatric physician and his three year old patient. But failure to communicate doesn't have to happen. As shown by my son's doctor, it can be intentionally and successfully avoided when individuals in charge of communication purposefully *explain the process* to be followed.

Predictably, the end result of my failed communication with Earl that day produced less than admirable outcomes. For the balance of that summer, I focused more of my time and effort on looking busy than on producing results.

So, what are we really trying to do when we focus on *explaining the process*?

When Explaining the Process...Understand Your Objective

Understanding how to *explain the process* better begins with understanding your overall communication objectives. There are at least six objectives from which to build successful communications. Ultimately, the communication we undertake may focus on just one of these objectives or any combination of them. But, knowing what your objectives are before you begin significantly lessens the chances that you will falter in your communication efforts that follow.

Consider the following communication objectives:

- **To convey.** Occasionally, we are truly just the messenger. At such times our job is to be the conduit through which information passes from one person or group to others.

- **To request.** There are occasions when our communication intent is to ask for something specific. Salespeople, for example, know that few deals are closed if the request is not made.

- **To educate.** Education is necessary for young and old alike. Before one can comfortably embrace a concept, idea or activity, some measure of focused education must prove its value and worthiness.

- **To defend.** People tend to see things from their own unique perspective. Therefore, situations arise when it becomes necessary to defend the ground (literally and philosophically) on which one stands.

- **To question.** It has been said that a question well formed is a problem half solved. Great communicators often are great question askers.

- **To confirm.** Building a reputation for transparent communication requires periodic validation of things known. Great communicators confirm whenever possible in order to erase doubts and confusion in the minds of others.

When Explaining the Process...Know What Others Sense

Communication is not only a verbal experience, in a very real sense it is also sensory in nature. People pride themselves on their ability to "read" other people. People evaluate their "gut feel" regarding messages they receive from others. People are always on the lookout for "a connection," "kindred spirits" and their "soul mate."

So what exactly do we mean by these sayings? Probably the sayings themselves mean different things to different people. But, I'm convinced there are at least six universal things that people can "sense" from our words and the manner in which we deliver them. Consider the following:

• **People can sense how you feel**. Are you enthused or embarrassed? Desperate or disgusted? Emboldened or embattled? The words you choose and the manner in which you deliver them give indication of all these possibilities and more.

• **People can sense if you like them or not**. Certainly there are times when we think people like us and they don't, and other times when we think they don't like us, but they do. Nevertheless, words can have a chilling effect on relationships.

• **People can sense if you're glad to be there**. We learn at an early age how to plaster on our "greeting line" smiles. Still, attentive, intuitive people can recognize these smiles for the masks they truly are.

• **People can sense if you've memorized your comments**. Memorization robs a message of its warmth and spontaneity. Think of the reason you are communicating a particular message, then *familiarize* yourself with that message, don't memorize it.

• **People can sense if you're lying**. Back in the 1970's, the pop music group, The Eagles, sang, *"you can't hide your lying eyes."* I believe they were right. Most people (thankfully) have not developed the pathological ability to lie with the same anatomical effect as telling the truth. When in doubt—tell the truth!

• **People can sense if you're trying to sell them something.** Most people want to *buy*, they don't want to be *sold*. Communicate the benefits clearly and highlight the value of that which you are communicating and there will be no need to try to sell people on anything. They will gladly "buy" what you are offering because they realize the worthiness of the thing.

• **People can sense if you're sincere.** Some people try valiantly to fake sincerity. Ultimately, however, their ill-fated attempts will leave them with more problems in their communication attempts than successes. Either be sincere in your efforts or quit pretending.

When Explaining the Process…Anticipate Key Questions

Let's face it, many of us are suspicious by nature. When someone starts "explaining the process" to us, we start trying to read between the lines. We wonder about a number of things. And until we have acceptable answers to questions that concern us, we will not be able to fully accept the communication effort as being legitimate. However, satisfy us with answers to our most pressing questions and we will value you as being the great communicator you are.

Consider the following questions that are common to people and then fashion an acceptable, customized response to each based on the varying circumstances and individuals involved. Remember the old saying, "Forewarned is forearmed." I am forewarning you now that these questions are important. So forearm yourself accordingly with answers that will help you *explain the process* sufficiently to others.

Questions to consider:

• *Is this really going to do any good?*

• *Is it possible that I could be hurt as a result of what happens?*

- *Should I get involved personally, or just watch and wait to see what happens?*

- *What is the real motivation behind what I am seeing and hearing?*

- *Will this have a negative effect on my relationship with _____?*

- *Will this cause more problems than it is worth?*

5

Principle # 3

Tell the Truth

Most of us were taught at an early age that "honesty is the best policy." As a father, I have reminded my children again and again that when troubles arise, it's always better to be truthful from the outset, than to complicate those problems with fabrications, misrepresentations and outright lies.

But let's face reality. As a child, it's one thing to be honest and own up to breaking a vase or intentionally leaving an assigned chore undone. But what about the types of problems we face as adults in our life and work? As we grow older and assume more personal and professional responsibility, the scope and breadth of the tribulations we encounter grow more complex. The problems which we are responsible for managing quickly expand to include superiors, subordinates, colleagues, clients, customers, creditors, regulators, investors, media, and so on.

In our hearts we continue to know that honesty is the best *policy*, but in our heads we wonder if honesty is the best *strategy*. When inevitably faced with a need to share an unpleasant, unwelcomed, uncomfortable message, we naturally begin to question whether or not being forthright is the right thing to do.

We ask ourselves questions like: Am I really the best one to share this message? Does this message need to be shared right now? Does this message need to be shared at all? What would it hurt to let others discover this information for themselves in due time?

When the need for honest, open communication is most critical, too often we hesitate and falter, when we should forge ahead. Why don't we? Because we simply don't trust our personal ability to communicate a difficult message or unpleasant information honestly and still be liked, appreciated and respected.

The third lesson the doctor so ably illustrated during his dealings with my son was that of the critical importance of honesty and truthfulness in every communication. This medical professional understood that to be believed, it was imperative that he *tell the truth*. I stood by and watched as the doctor looked deep into the eyes of my three year old and clearly stated, "Joe, this is going to hurt."

Now, even a three-year old could appreciate the personal implication of that message. Frankly, it was not a message that anyone would want to hear. But, it was certainly a message that needed to be heard. However, the doctor didn't just share his bad news and let the chips fall where they might. Yes, the doctor freely shared the unpleasant message, but then went on to explain in terms that Joe could easily understand, that the pain would be short-lived and that it was a necessary part of the healing process.

The doctor apparently knew what too many people seem not to know. He knew that telling people only what they *want* to hear may buy a little time initially. But in the end, it seldom, if ever, buys the results you want or the reputation you need—the reputation that identifies you as someone to be listened to and trusted.

I'll Tell You the Truth

So how does telling the truth, even under difficult circumstances, play out in a real world scenario? Sometimes it can be more than a bit uncomfortable.

It was mid-morning. I was working in my office. I was a Human Resources Manager for a FORTUNE 500 manufacturing company. I heard a knock at my door. I glanced up—there stood Harvey. I knew instinctively that whatever happened next would not be pleasant.

In keeping with our focus on truthfulness, before I go any further with this story, I must honestly admit to you that I didn't like Harvey. I imagine there have been people with whom you've worked, that you didn't especially care for either. Well, that was Harvey for me. In fact, out of more than 400 employees in our plant at that time, Harvey ranked toward the top of the list as one of my least favorite.

Harvey had never done anything to me personally. Overall, he was just a hard guy to like. One of the more senior employees in the workforce, Harvey was distant by choice, preferring to be alone most of the time. He had few friends and saw little need for conversation. When he did speak, his words could cut like a knife. He was caustic in his comments and negative in his outlook. Whenever workplace changes were announced—whatever they might be—Harvey was traditionally one of the most outspoken and adamant opponents. On those occasions during which he felt he had been wronged personally, he was quick to lash out with disgust and disdain. His favorite targets? Management!

The truth was inescapable. Harvey was simply not an easy guy to like. And on this particular occasion, Harvey didn't waste any time in declaring his intentions to me.

"I want to be transferred out of my department and I want out now!" Harvey declared forcefully.

Though I inherently expected the worst, I was still caught completely off guard by Harvey's demand. I didn't understand where he was coming from. Therefore, there was nothing for me to do but ask the obvious question.

"Why?"

"Because I'm sick and tired of working for that lying Butch. He just told me that I've been passed over for the lead person's position—for the third time! And again he told me that it was because there was a more experienced candidate. That's just a bold-faced lie! There's nobody in the department that's more experienced than me and Butch knows it. So that makes Butch a (expletive deleted) liar. And I told him so to his face. And I'll tell you one thing right now, too. I'm not gonna work for a (expletive deleted) liar!"

(As a brief explanation, the lead person position in our company was one level below a supervisor in the organizational hierarchy and one level above

an hourly worker's position—such as the one Harvey had occupied for years. Besides having the responsibility to order supplies, monitor inventory levels and document product quality problems, the lead person's job responsibilities also required a significant amount of on-going one-on-one interaction with all the employees throughout the department—something that Harvey's current position required none of.)

Harvey's words were venomous, harsh even for his standards. And they were also unacceptable. Even though he was obviously upset, I could not allow such malicious, slanderous comments to be made regarding another employee, especially his supervisor, without some sort of intervention. I knew a confrontation was inevitable. Nevertheless, I tried to maintain my cool as I did what I could to calm him down.

"Harvey, hold on a minute. I really don't know what you're talking about. But, I do know that I don't intend to sit here and let you call Butch names, especially when he's not here to defend himself. You say you've got a problem. Well, I'm willing to give your problem the attention it deserves. Just have a seat. I'll call Butch and have him join us and then we can all get to the bottom of this problem together."

Butch arrived in my office a few minutes later. As he walked in, I could tell from his facial expression and body language that he was already upset. He wouldn't even look in Harvey's direction. These two men were definitely at odds with one another. I sensed that a significant confrontation was brewing and probably had been for some time. At the time, I believed it was better to have that confrontation in a managed environment with some sort of mediator—me—than to have it erupt spontaneously out on the shop floor where other employees could watch, listen and possibly even become involved.

Still trying to maintain some semblance of professionalism and civility, I began by saying, "Butch, Harvey tells me that he thinks he has been wrongfully passed over for promotion in regard to your department's lead person position. Can you tell me about how you made your recent decision on the new lead person?"

Though obviously upset, Butch tried mightily to maintain his composure.

"A lead person's job came open and I looked around the department to see who I thought would be the best person for the job," Butch stated simply. "I considered several people, including Harvey, but I decided on Pete instead."

Without invitation, at this point Harvey jumped into the fray.

"Yeah, you decided on Pete. But it wasn't because he was the most experienced person in the department. You know good and well that's me. The truth is you promoted Pete because you didn't want me to have the position. Ain't that right? Go ahead. Tell the truth, if you can, for once in your life. I dare you."

Harvey's words were sharp and taunting. And it was obvious that they quickly found their mark. Butch had heard all he cared to hear. Before I could intervene, Butch had turned his full attention—and verbal fury—toward Harvey. His eyes flashed. His face reddened. And before my eyes I witnessed a scene play out that was eerily similar to the famous courtroom scene from the movie, *A Few Good Men*, where the prosecuting attorney played by Tom Cruise, on cross examination, so memorably demanded the truth from the Army Colonel portrayed by Jack Nicholson.

"You want to know the truth?" Butch began, his voice rising at least two octaves above normal. "Well, I'll tell you the truth. Here it is. I didn't promote you because I was sure that the longer I kept you away from the other employees in our department, the better off we all would be. Harvey, you make absolutely no effort to get along with or to get to know anybody in the department. As a result, nobody can stand working with you. When you do speak you are insulting, bordering on intimidating. No one wants to walk around on pins and needles, wondering what's going to set you off next.

"Harvey, nobody, including me, questions your ability, knowledge or commitment to doing a good job. It's you attitude that sucks. If you would just approach your job and the people you come in contact with a little more professionalism, you would've been the lead person in our department a long time ago. But, there's absolutely no way I'm going to put you in that position—now or ever—until I'm sure you will do more good than harm."

There it was—the truth—prominently displayed for all to see. It is what many had thought over the years and none had said, at least not directly to Harvey. Butch had laid all his cards on the table. Though obviously upset, he had shared his message while maintaining at least some measure of self-control. Still, there was no mistaking that Butch had meant what he said, regardless of how difficult it might have been for Harvey to hear or accept.

The entire time Butch was speaking, Harvey had stared, virtually emotionless, straight into Butch's eyes. With Butch's final words still hanging in the air, Harvey spoke up once more.

Still looking straight at Butch, Harvey asked pointedly, "So are you finally telling me the truth this time?"

"Yeah, I'm telling you the truth," Butch barked, staring straight back at Harvey. "I *believe* every word I said and I *meant* every word I said."

"Well then," Harvey responded, "if you're such a great supervisor, why did it take you this long to tell me what my problem was? Is this how you treat all of your employees? How are we supposed to get better if we don't know what you expect from us and what you are evaluating us on?

"Butch, I'm telling you right now, I want to be a lead person. And if it means I need to get along with people better, then that's what I'll do. You better watch me closely. Because the next time a lead person's position opens up, you won't have any excuses for not promoting me."

As a firsthand witness to the entire episode, I assure you the meeting ended with only slightly less tension than that with which it began. With Harvey gone, Butch and I spoke privately. We both agreed that Butch had said what needed to be said. But, Harvey's words stung us both… "If you're such a great supervisor, why did it take you so long to tell me what my problem was? Is that how you treat all your employees? How are we supposed to get better…?"

Harvey was right. We had not done our job as a supervisor and manager. We both had abdicated our professional responsibilities by avoiding what we both knew to be the truth regarding Harvey. He needed to know— deserved to know—much earlier, the truth about our perception of his abilities and shortcomings. There was no need for the problem to have grown and festered to the point it did before being addressed directly. Once again I was reminded—bad news doesn't get better with time. We simply should have counseled with Harvey sooner.

Nevertheless, neither of us expected any significant changes in Harvey's behavior. But we were wrong again. Relative to Harvey's professional behavior and performance from that point forward, something just short of amazing happened. In the weeks and months that followed the meeting in my office, as hard as it was for many of us to believe, Harvey underwent a professional transformation unlike anything I have seen before or since. Harvey was a changed man. It was obvious to all that he took his working relationships more seriously, while working hard at improving both his social and communication skills.

Now, we all know that Rome wasn't built in a day and Harvey didn't transform himself overnight. But Harvey did change and his personal transformation continued over time. And he changed for one reason and only one reason—he now knew the truth and he accepted it. A little more than a year later Harvey was promoted into his department's lead person's position. A few more years after that he was promoted again, by Butch, into Butch's supervisory position, as Butch moved into higher levels of management.

Is this an extreme example? Probably so. But it reminds us of the importance and value of honest, open, person-to-person communication. Let's face it. People may not always like or enjoy hearing the truth. But, without the truth, they have no opportunity to make decisions that improve their circumstance.

The Truth Shall Set Your Free

It seems like telling the truth ought to be a whole lot easier than it actually is. Of course, if all we ever did was share good news with others, then telling the truth would always be fun and easy. But as evidenced by the conversation between the doctor and my son, sometimes it falls to us to share news truthfully that may not be readily welcomed or appreciated by others. That doesn't change the fact that truth telling is necessary.

The good doctor won the trust of a young patient, in large part, by simply telling the truth. Remember, my son had never had stitches before this encounter and as a result, really had no idea what to expect. Had his doctor said, "Joe, this won't hurt a bit," Joe would have had no practical, experiential reason not to believe him. In fact, I suspect Joe would have believed that statement and everything else the doctor told him right up until the very instant when the cold steel of the needle pierced the raw flesh of his chin. At that split second, when those nerve endings came alive, conveying to the brain the undeniable message that pain was, in fact, being experienced—from that moment on Joe would have believed nothing—absolutely nothing—that the doctor had or would tell him. All credibility would have been lost and rightfully so.

And so it is with each of us and the way people react and respond to us. Playing fast and loose with the truth is a recipe for disaster. On the other hand, learning to share the truth—even uncomfortable truths—in a masterful way can strengthen the foundation on which a relationship is built in a way that nothing else can.

You may be wondering how you can become known far and wide as a "truth teller" without exception. Here are a few ideas to get you started.

When Telling the Truth...Fess Up, When You Screw Up

In establishing your believability quotient as a communicator there is simply nothing more important than telling the truth, the whole truth and nothing but the truth. But, if mistakes have been made, if the untruths have already been told—how does one go about *reestablishing* believability?

My advice—fess up.

Try as we might, we can never retract the words we've spoken or the deeds we've done. And excuses won't help (e.g., "I didn't know the microphone was on...," "My boss should have told me...," or "I was afraid of what she might think..."). Plausible explanations are poor substitutes for taking personal responsibility.

Far and away, the most important action we can take in rebuilding a fractured reputation is to take responsibility publicly and quickly for the mistakes we've made and the lies we've told. Begin by fessing up to the people who were impacted most directly by your untruths. Here are three steps that can be taken to begin making things right.

1) **Be totally honest about your dishonesty.** Don't complicate the problem by continuing to lie about your lying. Just swallow hard and get the truth out there.

2) **Be contrite.** Once the truth is out there, take your medicine, in whatever form it might come...discipline, public ridicule, humiliation, diminished status, severed relationships, financial loss, and so on. Don't try to blame or implicate others for your actions. You will never look good by trying to make someone else look bad. Accept the fact that you screwed up and then go ahead and take your licks.

3) **Recognize that most people have short memories and a desire to forgive.** What was done or said during a thoughtless moment may take months, even years to undo. However, if mistakes are handled honestly

and tactfully, the old axiom, "Time heals all wounds," generally proves to be true. Be patient—it may take time. It may take time for others to forget and time for you to remember just how valuable the truth is to one's reputation.

When Telling the Truth…Be Judicious With "Brutal Honesty"

The foundation building characteristic of well-intentioned honesty is one thing. The devastation that can be wrought by a malicious tongue set on destruction is something else entirely. In life, I have discovered there are few circumstances that call for unbridled, brutal honesty and even fewer individuals who can be on the receiving end of brutal honesty without having some sort of psychological after-effects.

Brutal honesty serves to tear down people, damage teams and sever relationships. Even when the truth is being told, if it is told in a way that disregards or diminishes the feelings of the one receiving the information, some level of harm and lasting hurt is almost certain to result.

The confrontation between Harvey and Butch detailed earlier in this chapter is one of those rare occasions where the person being spoken to honestly— but harshly, was able to internalize the message and find value in it. More often, the result is that offended individuals will lash out in an attempt to "get even" with the one who has been so brutally honest.

The reminder is simple. Choose wisely the manner in which you share information. People have long memories.

When Telling the Truth…Anticipate Emotions

Finally, let me remind you that human beings are emotional beings. As a result, the truth, be it positive or negative, when first heard, is certain to elicit any number of emotional responses. The truth can raise people to levels of exuberance or lower them to the depths of exasperation. To a great degree, the level of emotional response is in direct correlation to the expertise of the communicator. Communication done well can strengthen, enable, empower and enthuse. Communication done poorly can weaken, disable, encumber and exhaust.

6

Principle # 4

Work for Understanding

Have you seen this television advertisement concerning the newest weight loss remedy? A polished, though somewhat over exuberant announcer proclaims:

"Now, lose pounds while you sleep! Our team of international scientists, researchers and physicians have finally discovered the organic key that unlocks the human metabolic code.

Why deprive yourself of the foods you love? Why waste precious hours in monotonous aerobic exercise? Why subject yourself to punishing sit ups and crunches? There is no need! Eat, drink and be merry, for tonight you lose!

Our miracle drug, Turbo 43-7, is made of all natural ingredients, including the extract of roots from the ancient sadral tree found deep in the jungles of Central America. Two non-habit forming tablets, taken with 22 ounces of water just before bedtime and you are guaranteed to awake renewed, refreshed and lighter on your feet—all with absolutely no physical effort on your part!

And if you take advantage of this TV offer right now, we will send your first 90-day supply of Turbo 43-7… ABSOLUTELY FREE! All you pay is two equal installments of $24.95 to cover shipping and handling.

Don't miss this once in a lifetime opportunity to lose while you snooze! Operators are standing by."

Have you seen the ad? Of course you haven't. I just made it up. But its message and its promised outcome sounds so inviting, so alluring, so easy, that you may have caught yourself wishing it was true.

Losing weight is hard work. It takes effort, sacrifice, personal discipline and long term commitment. That's why so few people actually lose weight in the first place.

And so is becoming a great communicator. Wouldn't it be wonderful to hear a speech, read a book or listen to a podcast on the topic of communication just before you retire for the evening only to wake up the next morning to the transformational realization that overnight your interpersonal communication skills had improved drastically? An appealing thought? Sure. But, unfortunately it's nothing more than fanciful nonsense.

Meaningful communication, like weight loss, doesn't just happen overnight. Becoming an expert communicator takes real effort and requires some heavy lifting. But when the necessary effort is made and the lessons are well learned, the influence and impact that results from the efforts of expert communicators may be nothing short of phenomenal.

The doctor had obviously invested the time, energy and effort necessary to become a noteworthy communicator. As certainly as it took considerable time—even years—to study, practice and perfect his skills as a physician, it also takes time to study, practice and perfect our skills as communicators. A significant key in the on-going quest to be a masterful communicator is to stay focused on the desired outcome and to continuously *work for understanding*.

The Seaweed Tie

I was sitting in my downtown hotel room looking out the window at the Boston skyline. It was a gray, wet, uninviting day in Beantown and I was getting fidgety. I had shaved, showered, dressed, eaten breakfast, read the paper and reviewed my speech notes. Still, I had over two and a half hours before my scheduled noontime speech at the Copley Plaza Convention Center.

Since I had some time to kill, I decided to explore the subterranean tunnels that snaked their way from my hotel to the convention center. In case you haven't visited Boston and its tunnels, don't be fooled into thinking of them as dark, dank tunnels teeming with bats and pasty skinned spelunkers. Nothing could be farther from the truth.

These pedestrian tunnels offer convenience for those who live, work and play in Boston. This mesh of passageways beneath the city leads to and from a maze of governmental agencies, private office buildings, downtown hotels and of course, the sprawling Copley Plaza Convention Center. Their construction helped ease the transportation burden on the streets of Boston above. They also offered a welcome reprieve for weary pedestrians, who for too long had to brave the fickle weather conditions common to New England.

On this day, as I descended into the tunnels below the city, I was surprised to discover a cavernous marketplace, featuring small, bustling business establishments. Included were coffee shops, newspaper stands, sunglass huts, cell phone kiosks and nooks selling local delicacies such as New England clam chowder. Most of the people I encountered appeared to me to be professionals hustling through the aisle ways to their next business meeting or appointment. I, on the other hand, was just wandering aimlessly soaking in the atmosphere.

As I meandered up one corridor and down another, I eventually happened upon a small tie shop. Since I wear ties frequently in my work, I decided to pause momentarily and do a little harmless window shopping. I was by no means in the market for another tie, especially the kind of flamboyant, over-priced ties frequently found in such boutique shops. After all, I had three or four dozen seldom worn ties hanging in my closet at that precise moment.

But, I did need a place to kill some time and this looked like as good a place as any. I was just about to step inside when I began having second thoughts. It probably would be helpful for you to know that there are two things that I absolutely hate. The first thing I hate is *shopping*. Now I have no problem with *going* and *buying* something that I want or need. But, I see absolutely no redeeming value in spending hours (that often seem like days to me) wandering up one aisle and down another in store after store on the off chance that I might stumble upon some item that I simply can't live without.

As bad as I hate the act of shopping, I hate worse still overly aggressive salespeople trying to *sell* me something I haven't determined I want or need. This is one of the few things in life that grate on my nerves and quickly puts me into a very ill-tempered mood. I have learned that about myself over time. Therefore, as I stood outside the tie shop, I found myself engaged in a rather spirited game of internal tug-of-war.

The easy going part of me was saying, *Go on in, Phil. This will be a good place to spend a little time. You might as well check out the styles, check out the prices and then be on your way.*

However, the more pragmatic part of me was saying, *Phil, you better not go in there. You know how you are. You'll get in there and some zealous salesperson will start hounding you to buy a tie and the next thing you know you will have worked yourself up unnecessarily before your presentation. It's better to just keep moving.*

I doubt that I am the only one who experiences such periodic inner struggles. And why I ultimately opted to do what I did is still unclear to me. But this I know. For once, I didn't heed the warnings of my pragmatic self. I didn't keep moving. I stepped inside the store instead. But, I had my guard up.

"Good morning, sir. How are you this morning?"

As I entered the shop, I noticed the young woman standing in the middle of the sales floor. I guessed her to be in her early to mid-twenties. Her greeting was pleasant and non-threatening. Still, I had no intention of offering her even the slightest opening from which she might begin a high pressure sales pitch. I kept my response brief.

"I'm fine, thank you."

"Is there anything I can help you with?" she asked.

"No, I'm just looking," I said, intentionally choosing a matter-of-fact tone.

"That's fine. I'll be right here in case you have any questions. It would be my pleasure to serve you," she offered very professionally.

As I intentionally moved away from the young woman toward a rack of ties several feet removed from the cash register, I remember consciously thinking that I appreciated her approach. She was friendly and professional, but not overbearing. From my vantage point, that was a good combination. But I didn't dwell on the thought. Instead, in no more than a couple of minutes my mind was elsewhere, lost in a sea of images comprised of bright colors, wild patterns and inflated price tags.

"Sir, what brings you to Boston?"

The words snuck up on me and caught me off guard momentarily. It had been less than ten minutes or so since I had spoken with the sales clerk. Nevertheless, I was already lost in my own little world and had forgotten that I was not alone in this store.

"I'm sorry, what did you say?" I asked.

"Oh, I was just asking what brings you to Boston," the sales clerk offered again.

No longer feeling threatened by the thought of predatory sales intentions, I found myself ready for a little conversation.

"How do you know I'm not from here?" I asked good-naturedly.

"Sir, that's easy. When you first entered the store and I asked how you were this morning, you responded by saying, 'Fiiine.'"

As she spoke the word "fine" back to me, she did her best to mimic an exaggerated Southern accent.

"I've never heard that word pronounced with three syllables before," she teased. "One little word and I could tell immediately that you weren't from around here."

Her terrible impression of a Southern accent sounded as funny to me as I must have sounded to her. I caught myself laughing along with her.

"I'll give you credit, young lady. You're pretty observant," I admitted. "I'm in town visiting from Kentucky."

"Well, welcome to Boston. I notice you're dressed for business. Are you attending a convention here?"

"I'm not really attending one," I admitted. "But a little later this morning I'm scheduled to speak to a group that's having a convention in the Copley Plaza Convention Hall."

"Speaking? If you don't mind my asking, what do you do?" she asked curiously.

"No, I don't mind. I'm a professional speaker and author," I said.

"Really?" she said with an obvious measure of surprise in her voice. "A speaker? So you just go around the country and people pay you to talk?"

I laughed and said, "Well, I like to think it's a little more than that, but, basically, yeah, I guess that's what I do."

"So who are you speaking to today?" she continued.

"I'm speaking to a group of IBM employees."

"Wow, IBM. Everybody has heard of IBM. How many people will be in your audience?"

"I think they said they're expecting about two thousand," I responded.

"TWO THOUSAND PEOPLE!" she shrieked with great animation. "I would be terrified. Aren't you nervous?" she asked incredulously.

"Well, I wasn't," I laughed. "But, after talking with you maybe I should reconsider."

We both laughed again.

"Sir, forgive me for being so inquisitive, but I've never met a professional speaker before today. The thought of what you do intrigues me. Do you mind if I ask you what it takes to be a professional speaker?"

I had not stepped into that tie shop with a ready made answer to that question. However, like most people, I am flattered when someone shows interest in me and what I do and this conversation was proving to be no exception. So, I spontaneously fashioned and presented a brief description of what I thought it took to be a professional speaker.

"Well, to be a professional speaker," I began, "one must have a certain amount of expertise in a particular subject area."

From there, for the next couple of minutes, I continued offering additional professional speaking criteria as each instinctively occurred to me. Finally, as my wellspring of spontaneity was beginning to dry up, in true professional speaking style, I summarized.

"...and so those are the things that are necessary to becoming a professional speaker."

Throughout my entire monologue, the young lady's attention was transfixed on me. She seemed to be soaking in every word I was saying. Her body language gave every indication that she was truly interested in absorbing and understanding the subject matter at hand. She listened patiently until I had finished my summarization. It was at that point she asked yet another question.

"That's really interesting," she responded sincerely. "But, I'm curious. Is it possible that you might have left out at least one key consideration for being a professional speaker?"

Of course that possibility existed. I was making my answer up on the fly. But, I wasn't quite ready to admit that to her. Besides, her question now had me curious. I wanted to hear what she was thinking.

"Sure, it's possible that I might have omitted one. Which one do you think that might have been?" I asked trying to give the impression I already knew what she was going to say.

"Well, as important as all those things you mentioned are, I couldn't help but think that it was equally important that a professional speaker like yourself be unique," she offered thoughtfully.

Unique? Admittedly, I had not thought about the importance of uniqueness while giving my original answer. And her observation made good sense. It didn't take long at all for me to seize the thought and run with it.

"Yes, being unique is important," I responded. "It's important that speakers don't say the same thing, in the same way as others. You're absolutely right. Uniqueness is a critical element of professional speaking success. I'm sorry I failed to mention it earlier."

At that point the young woman looked at me and casually asked, "Sir, would you be so kind as to step over here for just a moment?"

I willingly followed without question as she led me to the other side of the shop, where she deliberately stopped in front of an isolated display of ties.

"Sir, what do you think of this tie?" she asked, directing my attention to one particular tie on display.

I looked the tie over with a critical eye. It was not my preferred style of tie. It was multi-colored with varying shades of blue, green, purple, white and yellow throughout. There was no defined pattern. It had a nondescript design featuring what could best be described simply as swirls with splashes of color. As for the tie's texture, there was something noticeably different about it as compared to those surrounding it. Honestly, there was really nothing in particular about the tie that I liked. However, I liked the sales person enough by this point that I did not want to be rude, so I answered her question in a rather neutral, noncommittal manner.

"It's an interesting tie," I offered with little conviction.

Apparently not put off by my answer, the young sales professional forged ahead gamely.

"Sir, as you were talking about what you do, it occurred to me that you might be interested in this tie. You see, this is a one-of-a-kind tie. There is no other tie like this in the world."

Her statement was so grandiose, so sweeping, so over the top, I felt I had no recourse but to challenge it.

"Stop right there," I said. "Don't try to tell me that this is the only tie like this in the world. I travel all the time and see these shops everywhere I go. I know that..."

I never got to finish my thought. The young woman boldly jumped back into the verbal fray with the intent to defend her statement.

"Sir, please forgive me. I don't mean to interrupt and be rude, but I must. I assure you there is no other tie like this one in the world," she stated definitively.

"How can you make such a statement?" I asked.

"Sir, I can't explain all of it, but I certainly can explain some of it," she said as she casually took the tie from the display and placed it in my hands. "Sir, you're holding a rare seaweed and silk tie. This particular tie has been created in a small manufacturing center located in Northern Italy. It's made from a process that combines the finest Italian hand woven silk with, as strange as it might sound, seaweed harvested from the floor of the Mediterranean Sea. I must admit, I don't really know how they're able to combine the two, but when they do, each tie that's produced has its own distinctive color, pattern and texture, totally unlike any other tie anywhere."

The young woman paused ever so briefly to let her explanation take root. Then, looking me directly in the eye, she added with a great air of confidence, "Sir, I just thought a one-of-a-kind speaker ought to own a one-of-a-kind tie."

(Sigh)

I'm not going to tell you how much I paid for that tie. I will say it was more than I had ever paid for any tie before. But, I will also quickly add that I didn't begrudge the purchase.

You may very well be thinking at this point, "Phil, don't you realize that girl *sold* you that tie?" But I would argue that point. As I said earlier, the last thing I needed was another tie. But I gladly and with free will *bought* that tie not because I needed another tie, but because I wanted and needed what that young woman led me to realize that tie represented.

Again, I'm not ready to admit that that intuitive young woman *sold* me that tie. I knew what she was doing and I knew what I was doing all along. However, I will admit that she sold me something. She sold me on a concept. And she did so by masterfully communicating the importance of uniqueness and how that uniqueness impacted me personally. Once I had bought into that concept, the tie itself (along with its inflated purchase price) was nothing more than an afterthought.

Communicating is Hard Work

Though I'm quite sure the young woman selling ties and the doctor treating my son never met each other, I'm just as convinced they shared a unique quality. The best communicators are always willing to *work for understanding*. Some might believe the key word in that phrase is understanding —and understanding certainly is important. However, I would argue that the key word here is actually *work*. The doctor attending to my son's needs had probably administered thousands of stitches in his medical career— maybe tens of thousands. But, these were the first for my son. Everything about the experience was new. Recognizing that people learn and process information in different ways and at different speeds, this doctor's methodical process allowed him to understand exactly what my son did and did not understand—and to know what future steps had to be taken as a result of that knowledge.

Similarly, the young sales person knew her ties. What she didn't know was her individual customer's wants, needs, concerns, preferences, biases and so on. She had to *work* to garner that information and then use it to satisfy both the needs of her customer (me), as well as her own professional needs and objectives.

If, for just a moment, you can take the thought of medical school and all those years of medical practice out of the equation, I think you, like me, can easily imagine our doctor successfully selling ties and our young tie sales person successfully attending to the needs of patients. Why? Because they both exhibited the gift and developed skill of being able to work for understanding in their chosen fields of endeavor.

Working to understand the needs of others and working to be understood is a transferable skill, not limited to a specific professional discipline or activity. It is a skill both needed to be successful in their chosen professional venues. And it is a skill that the rest of us need as well. Being willing and able to *work for understanding*, to improve personal communication is needed, recognized and valued in the operating room, in the show room, in the classroom, in the boardroom and even in the living room.

Consider the following ways to *work for understanding*.

When Working for Understanding…Check the Pulse

There is always a right time and a wrong time, a right place and a wrong place, a right way and a wrong way to communicate. Great communicators are the ones who have come to realize that with successful interpersonal communication "one size does *not* fit all." As a result they work to fashion a tailored, customized communication message for those who will be receiving it. To accomplish this, proactive communicators need to have their finger on the pulse of those who will be impacted (positively or negatively) by the communication offered.

Here are some questions to consider as you formulate the specific message to be conveyed.

- *What are the key issues s/he is currently facing that can impact his/her reaction or response?*

- *Has s/he ever heard or dealt with this type of message before?*

- *If so, how has s/he reacted to it?*

- *How does this person handle good/bad news?*

- *What kind of things have we dealt with together in the past that could resurface (for good or bad) during our time of communication?*

When Working for Understanding…Anticipate and Manage the Barriers

A major part of good one-on-one communication is being able to anticipate and manage the numerous barriers that continuously crop up throughout any focused communication effort. Consider the following categories of barriers and the proactive suggestions offered to avoid them.

Sender Barriers

• **Intention.** Any successful journey begins with a well-defined itinerary. Communication is no different. The originators of the communication—the senders—need to be crystal clear on the intention of the communication to follow. As the old saying goes, "If you don't know where you're going, any road will take you there."

• **Preparation.** Once the intention is clear, the preparation must follow. There is absolutely no excuse for a lack of preparation on the part of the one who initiates communication. Consciously prepare for who you will be speaking with, what you want to accomplish and how best to present your ideas or information so that they can be well-received by your intended audience.

- **Singular Focus.** So as not to confuse those to whom our message will be delivered, the primary focus must remain clear and uncluttered. Focus on the "first things first." Don't try to cover too much ground or mix too many varying messages. It confuses the receiver of the communication. Stay true to the following format:

  - *Introduction:* Tell them what you are going to tell them.

  - *Body:* Tell them what you need to tell them.

  - *Conclusion:* Tell them what you just told them.

Receiver Barriers

- **Timeliness.** As the originator and sender of the message, do everything in your power to align and deliver the message in a timely fashion. A message received well in advance of its application is soon mentally discarded and forgotten. A messaged received too late is looked on with disdain.

- **Opportunity to Vent.** There is an emotional element to almost every message. As the originator of that message, it is imperative that you recognize that emotions and personal feelings are to be acknowledged and dealt with. As such, allowing receivers an opportunity to vent their thoughts and emotions adds to the value of the communication process.

- **Accept Responsibility.** As the sender of the communication, if and when you fail in some area of the communication process, be willing to accept responsibility for your failure quickly and publicly. Receivers will be much more apt to forgive and move forward when they recognize that you are accepting responsibility for your mistakes.

Message Barriers

- **Isolate the Problem.** Well meaning communication can often go awry when the intended message strays from the *problem* to the *person*. People will always defend themselves against perceived personal attacks.

Effective communicators have learned to isolate the problem and separate it from the people involved.

• **Procrastination.** On those occasions when it becomes necessary to communicate a message that is expected to be received negatively, too many communicators shrink from the challenge. They hope there will be a "better time" for such communication. Remember, "bad news does not get better with time." Don't procrastinate—communicate!

• **Communicate Expectations.** Any message can be misconstrued if it remains unclear as to what is expected to happen next. As the originator of the communication, it is your responsibility to conclude every exchange with your own personal "call to action." Make sure every person knows what is expected of them from that point forward.

Environmental Barriers

• **Appropriate Time.** As a general rule, if you are communicating a message that will be well-received and roundly supported, it is better to share that information as early in the day, the week, the month as possible. The positive buzz can have a desirable after-effect on others.

• **Privacy Matters.** On the other hand, if you expect a message you are called to communicate might have a negative backlash, plan to communicate that message out of the sight of prying eyes and ears. It is better to deal with unpredictable emotions in private.

• **Shut Down the "Grapevine."** Most organizations have some sort of informal, internal communication "grapevine" that too often dispenses rumors, speculation, innuendo and half-truths. Expert communicators can virtually shut down such grapevine communication by becoming known as the repository for dependable communication. Be proactive in making people's unknowns—known.

When Working for Understanding…Inspect What You Expect

Even the best planned, best prepared and best delivered message can, on occasion, be misconstrued unintentionally. But how can you know that, short of waiting for the whole issue to blow up in your face at a later time and place? You can always "test your message."

It's fairly simple. Here's what you do. Once you have communicated your intended message to the appropriate individual, before parting company you ask the following question, "I realize that I am not always the best communicator. I'm trying to get better. But, what we have just talked about is so important that I want to make sure that I have not done anything to confuse the message. Will you please tell me what you heard me say and what you know I am expecting as a result of our conversation today?"

Once you have asked this question, I suggest you stop and listen carefully to what is retold. Notice in the question above, I have worked hard to put the burden on the sender, not on the receiver of the message (i.e., "…I am not always the best communicator. I'm trying to get better…I want to make sure I have not done anything to confuse the message.") Therefore, if, in the repeating of the message back to you, the receiver gets something in message wrong, be sure to accept the blame for the confusion. Example: "Did I say that you have $5,000 in your budget for the next quarter? Oh my, I meant to say $500. Thanks for catching my mistake. That could have been disastrous."

Or another example. "Can you tell me once again what time I want you to have my daughter home from the dance?" "Oh, did I say midnight? I meant to say 11:00 p.m. Thank you for catching my mistake. That could have been unpleasant for all of us."

In a nutshell, *working for understanding* always takes work—but it can also bear great results.

7

Principle # 5

Get Others Involved

Consider briefly the overall process our insightful doctor followed as he intentionally and methodically established a communication platform with our three-year old son. His reason for doing so was clear. He recognized that he was dealing with a young, inexperienced patient in need of specific medical services. These services, by their very nature, would be seen as unpleasant and undesirable. The doctor knew that. Therefore, this M.D. found himself in a rather undesirable position. Nevertheless, he spent the first part of his interaction with Joe, utilizing a deft touch in both word and deed. The result? He did a remarkable job of establishing positive rapport from the outset.

But, as the process continued to unfold, what the doctor did next was both unexpected and exceptional. He asked for help. But, he didn't ask for help from me, or from my wife or even from the nurses in the examination room. The doctor turned his full attention to his young patient and asked him directly for his help.

Now, I'm not a psychologist, so I would be hard pressed to explain or defend all the psychological underpinnings regarding the concept of teamwork. Esteemed educators and intellectuals might be able to offer scientific evidence as to why people tend to better accept, support and defend that which they helped create or that with which they were personally involved. I admit I can't explain it. Frankly, I'm not even convinced that the doctor could have explained it.

But, whether the doctor could have explained it or not, there was one thing he understood clearly that I didn't at the time. He knew practically that if his patient was thinking *more* about a specific task assigned him, that same patient would be thinking *less* about the pain and discomfort he was experiencing. On the other hand, if the patient had nothing to focus on but the pain and discomfort, his natural reactions would be very different.

Expert communicators have long recognized the value of *getting others involved*. The more involved they are, the more successful the communication and outcomes. Joe's doctor was just one example. Here is another.

I Hired Him

More than twenty five years ago, I was working as a Human Resources Manager. The company I worked for produced fork lifts used in manufacturing environments and warehouses around the world. It was the early 1980s and my boss had given me the charge to introduce employee involvement activities and participative management techniques into our very traditional manufacturing operation.

At the time, our company was in the midst of introducing a new product. The increased production volume the new line represented meant we would need to hire approximately 125 new employees over the next eight to twelve months in order to staff the line properly. From my past experience in interviewing and selection, I knew that to fill 125 jobs I would need to conduct almost 400 separate interviews. In other words, I would need to interview three well-screened candidates in order to find one employee qualified to meet our exacting standards. My work was cut out for me. But it got even more challenging. My boss, Jerry, the Director of Human Resources, called me into his office.

"Phil, are you ready to begin interviewing for the production line jobs," Jerry asked.

"Jerry, I'm getting there. Right now I'm in the midst of advertising the job openings in the surrounding areas. The applications and resumes are beginning to trickle in. I should be ready to start the actual interviewing process in two, maybe three weeks."

"Good. You are planning to use some sort of participative technique as part of the interviewing process, aren't you?"

The thought had not even crossed my mind. I had been busy the previous several months extolling the virtues of participative management to managers and supervisors alike, most of whom were suspicious of the idea. They weren't particularly interested in relinquishing any authority or personal control to anybody—especially to hourly employees. But during the process, I had not paused long enough to realize that this might be a perfect opportunity to model participative management for those who might be on the fence regarding its value.

"Jerry, honestly, I hadn't even thought about it," I admitted.

"Well, I think you should think about it, don't you?"

Jerry's question was more a directive than a question and I knew it. I started working immediately to create a "team interviewing" format.

As far as I could tell, no one in our plant had ever participated in a team interview—either as interviewer or as interviewee—including me. Therefore, I built the concept from scratch, selling the idea, as best I could, along the way. First, I determined that every new hire would be interviewed and selected by a team of four interviewers. Though the interviewing teams would rotate once the positions assigned them had been filled, the defined makeup of the teams would remain the same. There would always be a representative from Human Resources, the department supervisor and two hourly employees, each possessing some measure of practical knowledge of the job to be filled (i.e., welders would interview perspective welders, assemblers would interview perspective assemblers, secretaries would interview perspective secretaries and so on). It was a brand new concept for all of us and as such, threatening for some. Front line supervisors especially hated the idea for two basic reasons.

First, they didn't like the idea of others—especially hourly employees—having a say in hiring individuals that the supervisor alone would ultimately be required to supervise. Secondly, they didn't like the idea of taking hourly employees away from their production jobs for extended periods for the purpose of participating in interviews. Nevertheless, the decision was made and we moved forward with the implementation of that decision.

Since the decision to move forward with team interviewing was already controversial, I knew it was vital that the initial members of the interviewing teams be of the highest quality—especially the participating hourly employees. I set about the task of trying to choose my "dream team" for team interviewing. The very first person that came to my mind was Darnell.

Darnell was in his early 30's and had worked at the plant for several years. He worked in the painting department, but was experienced in sanding and assembling as well. Since most of the new hires would be starting as sanders, I knew I wanted Darnell on the team—if only he would agree to participate.

As word spread throughout the plant that hourly employees might be invited to participate in interviewing job candidates, several hourly employees had gone on record as saying they would not participate for a number of different reasons—they didn't want the responsibility, they didn't want to go through the training, they didn't want to do work the supervisor ought to be doing and so on. I honestly didn't know where Darnell stood on the subject. I hoped he wouldn't be a "hard sell."

"Darnell, have you heard about this new team interviewing approach we're introducing?" I shouted over the considerable racket being made by the electrostatic paint booth in which he was working.

"Yeah, I've heard something about it," Darnell shouted back.

"I was wondering if you would be interested in participating on the first team we form?"

"Yeah, go ahead and mark me down. Just let me know what I need to do," was Darnell's simple and immediate reply.

"Will do," I said happily as I checked his name off my list and walked away.

Thank goodness. That was much easier than I expected, I thought.

About two weeks later, the first interviewing team in the history of our company convened for the purpose of beginning face-to-face interviews. As planned, the group consisted of two hourly employees (of which Darnell was one), the department supervisor and me. We had intentionally kept the team's training and orientation simple. In a previous session, I had instructed the group as to the type of questions we could and could not legally ask. I briefed them on the importance of maintaining confidentiality. I encouraged the individual members of the team to participate actively, not passively, in each and every interview. The only hard and fast rule we set for ourselves was that we would not offer a job to any candidate that the entire team did not unanimously approve.

The interviews began. I was impressed with the seriousness with which all of the team members took their responsibilities. During the interviews, the questions of candidates and attentiveness to their answers was good. Following each interview, the discussion of each candidate and what they might bring to the job was spirited. It was obvious that each team member was giving their best effort.

That first day we interviewed four candidates for one available sander position. For one reason or another, we were unable to unanimously agree on any one of the four. At the end of the first day of interviewing, I thanked each team member for their effort and contribution, and reminded them I would be lining up more candidates for their consideration the next day.

Day two arrived with four more candidates available. Again, the team assembled, conducted interviews and finished without agreeing on a single candidate. By this point, I had noticed a pattern had begun to reveal itself. Though none of the candidates had been exceptionally strong, I felt that some of them would have been passable as employees. In fact, two other members of the team felt the same way I did. But, again and again, the lone hold out was Darnell. Darnell showed no hostility or animosity. He didn't seem to enjoy wielding the veto power that comes with casting the lone dissenting vote. On the contrary, I heard him say again and again, "He/she was okay, I guess. But, I really think we can do better."

By the time the third day of interviews rolled around I was concerned. Remember, my past interviewing experience had yielded a 3:1 interviews to hire ratio. So far with the new interviewing format we were 0 for 8.

What if this trend continues? I have 125 positions to fill. What if we haven't even filled one after three days of interviewing? Is this process flawed? Did I make a mistake suggesting it? How much longer until the supervisors and managers begin to grumble, then revolt? What will Jerry think about my failure to make this system work? How will this make me look? Why isn't Darnell on board with this thing? I've got to do something before this whole thing falls apart. I need to talk to Darnell.

I called Darnell and asked him to meet with me privately a few minutes before the other team members were scheduled to arrive. Darnell agreed.

"Darnell, what do you think of the new interviewing process so far?" I asked choosing to ease into this uncomfortable discussion.

"I think it's gonna be really good," he said simply.

"Well, Darnell, I thought so, too. But, I've got to admit, I'm a little concerned at this point. We've interviewed eight decent candidates so far. But, you've found something wrong with each one. I'm just wondering, is it possible that you've set your personal standard a little too high?"

Darnell looked at me for several seconds before responding. When he spoke he had my full attention.

"Phil, do you remember that day when you came out on the plant floor and asked if I'd be interested in participating in these team interviews?"

"Yeah, I remember. You were the first one I asked and I was thrilled that you said 'yes.' I still am," I said honestly.

"Phil, do you remember what questions I asked you about the process at the time?"

I thought for a moment.

"Darnell, I don't honestly remember you asking me any questions."

"That's right. You don't remember me asking any, because I didn't ask any. Phil, I've worked in this plant for eight and a half years. I can't tell you how many times I have been working at my station and I either heard about or watched decisions being made that made absolutely no sense to me. I've said to myself over and over again, 'If I was the one making the decisions around here, things would be different.'

"Then out of the blue you come out and ask me to serve on this interviewing team. Phil, whether you know it or not, you're the first person that has ever asked me to contribute with my head and not just with my hands in almost nine years with this company. I said 'yes' without any hesitation because I saw this as my opportunity to do something for this company that will last for a long time.

"Yeah, some of the folks we've interviewed so far have been 'decent' and they probably would've done a 'decent' job. But I've decided if my name is gonna be associated with this person we hire, I want somebody who is more than just decent. I want somebody who'll make this place better and who I can be proud of."

Darnell's voice was calm and measured throughout. There was no trace of bitterness or anger at all. His words were thoughtful and spoke of passion and reason. He was successful in communicating his bigger vision of not what the company *was* but rather what the company *could* be.

As I listened to Darnell, I realized just how selfish I had been. Darnell was concerned with making the company better. I was concerned with making myself look good—or at least keeping myself from looking bad. I was willing to settle for *decent*. Darnell was unwilling to settle for anything less than *better*.

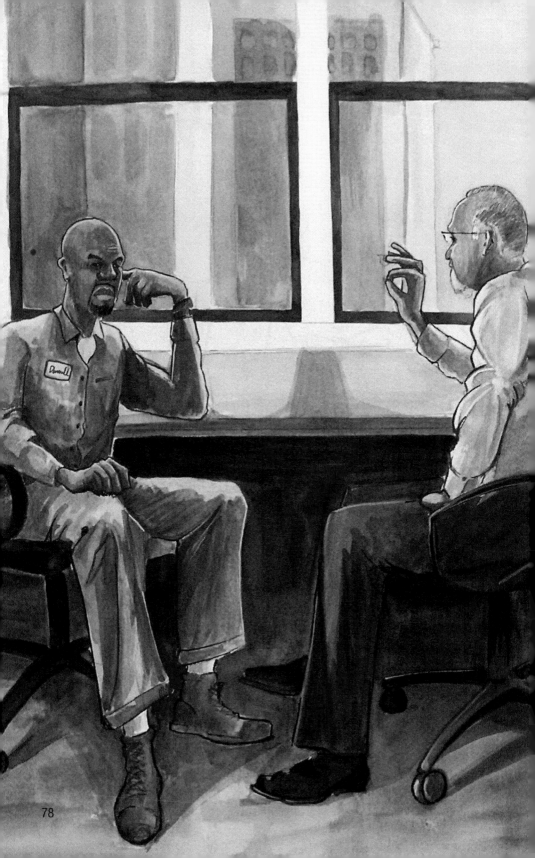

I looked across the table at Darnell and apologized.

"Darnell, I'm sorry. You're right. As a manager, I should be the one that's setting the bar higher. But since I didn't, I'm glad you did. I promise to support you and everyone else on this team until we can all be satisfied with our choice—even if it takes two dozen interviews."

Later that afternoon, candidate number twelve, got a unanimous vote of approval from all of us on the interviewing team. We all agreed that he was a notch above the other candidates we had interviewed. Candidate number twelve accepted the position that was offered him. The interview team was thanked for their service and released from their obligation to return to their normal responsibilities.

About three weeks later, I was walking through the plant and I found myself passing the paint booth adjacent to the sanding area. Over the din of the machines, I heard someone shouting my name. I looked up to see Darnell standing atop a fork lift in the paint booth. Darnell's flailing arms made me know he had something he wanted to tell me. I stood, waiting patiently for several minutes as climbed down from the fork lift and as he freed himself from all the safety apparatus. When he finally made his way to me I could see a huge smile creasing his face.

"Hey, Darnell, what's up?" I shouted as he drew closer.

With the fixed smile still in place, Darnell shouted back, "I just wanted to know if you have been keeping up with our boy's progress?" he said, as he gestured toward candidate number twelve who was sanding a fork lift across the way.

"To be honest, I've been pretty busy lately and I haven't checked up on him. How's he doing?" I asked.

"He's doing great! In fact, I've decided he's the second best sander the company has ever had," Darnell declared definitively.

"Is that right? Second best? Who's the best?" I asked.

"Me! That's who," Darnell said as he threw his head back and laughed loudly. He then looked at me and smiled broadly once more.

"And Phil, you know what the best part of the whole thing is? I hired him!"

Striving for Heightened Involvement

When someone is offered the opportunity to get involved, any number of things can happen. She may reject the offer out of hand for any number of stated reasons or for no conceivable reason whatsoever. Some people are like that. They don't want to step out at all. They want the comfort and security of knowing exactly what they will be doing and what is expected of them. No amount of encouragement or harassment will be sufficient to change her mind.

Others might consider and accept your offer of heightened involvement, only to renege and back away as the time for active involvement approaches. There will always be those who fear commitment and who lack the willingness to follow through, even though they may initially talk a good game.

Both types of individuals can frustrate those of us who are striving to be better communicators and who are consciously trying to follow the lead of folks like Joe's doctor by simply *getting others involved* in the overall communication process. They can be so frustrating that you might be tempted to throw your hands up in frustration and ask yourself, "What's the use?"

To surrender, to quit, is to acknowledge defeat. And though not everyone possesses the psychological makeup to accept heightened levels of involvement when offered them, some do. People like Darnell and my son. And when they do choose to get involved some pretty amazing things can result—things you probably would never predict. All because you didn't abandon your opportunity to *get others involved*.

Consider the following tips to get others more actively and personally involved in the communication process.

When Getting Others Involved…Ask Their Preference

One of the best ways to get others involved is by asking a fairly open-ended question such as, "What would you like to see happen from this point forward?" or "If you had your way what direction would you have us go and why?"

As mentioned before, not everyone will immediately embrace personal involvement. However, some will. And when they do choose to respond to the type of question offered above, it is very easy then to move to the next step. The next step involves extending a personal invitation to become more personally involved in the actions to be taken or decisions to be made.

Darnell had been standing at his work station for more than eight years waiting and wishing for someone to ask him what he thought and to invite him to get involved. When the invitation was extended he responded.

My son's circumstance was different than Darnell's. He didn't know what to think about his surroundings. Everything was strange and new. However, his opportunity to get involved revolved around the concept of accepting the challenge of rising to "big boy" status. Joe was willing to accept the responsibilities that came with that distinction.

How many Darnells and Joes are there around you? Probably more than you think. But, you'll never know for sure unless you ask.

When Getting Others Involved…Be Specific

When offering the chance to get others involved, too often the tendency is to leave the activity open-ended. That's a bad idea. Few people will reach blindly into a bag unless they have some idea what is in that bag already. Not knowing creates fear, anxiety and hesitancy.

It's much better to tell people *specifically* what they are getting into and what is expected of them. I told Darnell that I wanted him to serve on an interviewing team until we were able to hire the right person to fill the available opening. Though there were still some questions to be answered, Darnell knew the scope and duration of what he was agreeing to be involved with.

Similarly, the doctor told Joe that he needed for him to lie still on the table, keep his hands under his butt and keep his chin in the air—three very specific activities that even a three-year old boy could understand and agree to.

As it relates to communication, specificity rules!

When Getting Others Involved…Recognize Success

Once you are successful in getting others more actively involved, there is one more key activity that should not be overlooked. Catch people doing things right and recognize their successes in every way possible.

It takes courage to step out on faith and to take on additional responsibility. Over time, the more involved people become, the more communicative they become. Fewer problems occur when people are talking to one another. So, we should be doing all that is within our power to keep people talking.

Show people what success looks like. Trumpet the successes that you are observing. Don't wait for huge, "front page news" successes. Be just as quick to acknowledge and highlight the "look, we've made a little progress" successes, too.

The personal involvement of others is a skill not easily mastered, but one that can pay significant future dividends.

Principle # 6

Do Your Job

The sixth communication principle the doctor practiced with Joe, initially went unnoticed by me, and therefore, almost went unrecorded.

When I first sat down to analyze all that had transpired following Joe's accident and the subsequent medical treatment he received, I naturally focused on the key communication principles I had observed the doctor practicing. I watched and listened as he masterfully *talked with people*, as he carefully *explained the process*, as he recognized the need to *tell the truth*, as he *worked for understanding* and as he was diligent in *getting others involved* throughout the process.

As I sat and relived the experience over and over in my mind, I was confident I had identified and captured all the things I had watched the doctor do. But as I reviewed these five principles, I had this gnawing feeling that something was missing. I felt as if something had been overlooked. Suddenly, a thought struck me:

I saw what the doctor did. But, what if things had not gone so well?

With that new line of thinking banging around in my head, I took pen in hand again and this time wrote in big letters lower on the page: WHAT IF...?

- *What if...things had not gone the way they did?*
- *What if...things had gone badly?*
- *What if...my wife and I had become too meddlesome?*
- *What if...my wife and I had become too protective of Joe?*
- *What if...my wife and I had become too emotional?*

- *What if...Joe had resisted the doctor's communication efforts?*
- *What if...Joe had become aggressive and combative?*

After considering these and other "What if...?" questions for a while, I came to the realization that none of us can predict with certainty what the outcome of any communication effort ultimately will be. We can know what we want the outcome to be. We can know what we have planned the outcome to be. We can even know what we have intentionally worked for the outcome to be. But in the end, we simply don't control all the variables.

It was then that the sixth communication principle came into focus for me. I realized that whatever happens in the course of our communication efforts—good or bad—the people who are depending on us still expect us to *do our jobs*. That's why Susan and I immediately loaded Joe into the car after his accident and drove him to the doctor's office in the first place. We needed the professional services of a doctor.

Susan and I never considered for an instant the possibility of sitting Joe in a chair at home and sewing his chin up ourselves. Ridiculous! We weren't trained to do such work. We weren't experienced in doing such work. We weren't emotionally prepared to do such work. That wasn't our job. No, we knew that we needed to get Joe to a doctor. Whatever happened once we arrived at the doctor's office, we were confident the doctor would be able to handle it. We expected the doctor to do his job and he did.

Consider just one of the above "What if...?" scenarios. What if Joe had become aggressive and combative as the doctor was talking with and preparing him for the treatment to follow? Do your really think the doctor would have thrown his hands in the air and said to me, "I'm sorry Mr. Van Hooser. Joe is not listening very well this morning and he won't lie still on the table as I have repeatedly asked him to do. Therefore, I'm afraid you will just have to take Joe to another doctor for treatment." I seriously doubt it. I think it's more realistic to expect the conversation to have gone more like this. "Mr. Van

Hooser, as you can see, Joe is not being very cooperative. Nevertheless, that chin must be repaired. Therefore, we need to shift to Plan B. Nurse, will you please bring in the restraining apparatus?"

Despite hating the thought of my son being restrained, I would have actually had more respect for the doctor in the second scenario than in the first. Why? Because we all recognize that things don't always go exactly as planned. We all recognize that not every part of our job is fun. And we all recognize we have people counting on us to do for them what they want and need done. Deep down in all of us there is an abiding respect for people who do their job well, despite unpleasant, uncomfortable or unfortunate circumstances.

What Do You Think?

A few years ago, while in the process of preparing a speech for a group of operating room nurses, I asked a friend, who happened to be a cardio-thoracic surgeon, if I could shadow him for a day in the operating room. He was beside himself with enthusiasm. He loved the idea and agreed to my request with no hesitation.

On the appointed day, the doors of the operating room swung open as the surgical team entered, with me in tow. At their direction, I took my place atop a box at the head of the patient, directly beside the anesthesiologist.

For the next six hours I stood in rapt attention watching my friend and his equally skilled colleagues work their medical magic on three separate patients—one requiring double bypass heart surgery, one requiring carotid artery surgery and the third requiring a lung biopsy. From my perch, I witnessed things firsthand that I had only previously read about. For example, I watched in awe as my buddy gently held a human heart in the cup of his hand before returning it to his patient's chest cavity.

But as impressive as these observations were, even more impressive was the skill, precision and professionalism that I observed from those working at literally every angle around the patient. Without question, this was a team at work. A well trained team. A well ordered team. A well respected team. A highly communicative team.

When the final procedure was complete, my surgeon friend backed away from the operating table. He motioned for me to join him. I climbed down off my box and made my way to his side. As I approached, he lowered his surgical mask, revealing a broad, toothy smile. It was obvious to all of us—he was in his element, he was having fun, he loved his job. Almost breathless in anticipation of my answer, John asked me the question I was sure he had wanted to ask all day.

"So, Phil, what do you think?"

It was hard to know how to answer. I had thought so many things in the preceding hours. I had witnessed firsthand things that few people outside the medical profession ever would. It was truly overwhelming.

"John, it was amazing. I've never seen anything like that in my life. Every person in this room is so totally focused. It's hard to comprehend this level of performance excellence," I said, realizing I was unintentionally beginning to gush. John and those around him didn't seem to mind. John continued to beam with pride.

We stood and talked for a couple of minutes more. Then without warning, I watched as John's demeanor changed right before my eyes. His shoulders seemed to sag a bit. The broad smile left his face. His eyes found the ground.

"Now comes the hard part of my job," he muttered.

John's nonverbal cues in concert with his words led me to assume the worst. With no real foundation on which to base my assumption, still I found myself wondering if John had lost a patient and if it was now his responsibility to address the family and to console them in their loss. I could only imagine how difficult a task that might be.

"What do you have to do, John?" I asked hesitantly, seeking clarification.

John looked up at me with a weary look.

"Now I have to spend the next two hours talking to patients," he responded flatly.

I was shocked. John's words caught me totally by surprise. There was no deceased patient. John had just spent the better part of six hours hunched over an operating room table, performing some of the most delicate and intricate procedures ever devised by medical scientists. He literally held the power of life and death in his hands. And guess what? That was the part of the job he loved most. That was the part that he had spent years in classrooms and in residency perfecting. The part of his job he dreaded was the routine, on-going interpersonal part. That, too, was part of his job. It just didn't happen to be the "stuff" that he loved.

What Do You Love Most?

So what is the "stuff" that you don't enjoy doing in your job? Does it involve on-going communication?

I happen to know that John is an above average communicator. But, for the sake of argument, let's assume that he is a horrible communicator. Maybe his unique credentials, experience and reputation as a world class heart surgeon, in an industry where technical skill is highly valued, would be enough to keep him at the top of his career despite his significant limitations as a communicator. But I seriously doubt that very many of the rest of us have such a luxury. We are who we are and what we are—in large part, good or bad—based on the level of our communication skills. The more accomplished our communication skills, the more personal and professional opportunities that come our way. Conversely, the less skilled we are as communicators, the more opportunities drift from us to those who have learned to communicate better interpersonally.

It is human nature to be drawn to those activities that excite us, inspire us and fulfill us. But life and work is not always exciting, inspiring and fulfilling. Sometimes you are called to rise above that which you wish you could avoid completely. Joe's doctor readily accepted that responsibility himself as he went about doing his job as professionally as possible. The results of his efforts with this patient were more than I could have possibly imagined. All of your personal and professional activities can be enhanced as well if you simply commit yourself to doing your job and doing it at the highest level possible.

Here are three ideas on how to get better.

When Doing Your Job…Strive to Become A Better Communicator

One way to become a better communicator is happening for you at this very moment—you're reading and studying. Though reading this book or others is no guarantee that you will be ordained the next great communicator. It is, however, a wonderful step in the right direction. Self-study serves to prepare the mind and will for greater future accomplishment.

My intention here is not to burden you with a suggested reading list as long as your arm. If you are really interested in more reading materials related to communication skills enhancement, fifteen minutes spent in your local library, bookstore or online will provide you dozens of options. I will suggest one book in particular though that I think can be helpful to anyone at any stage of their life or career. Secure a copy today of Dale Carnegie's classic, *How to Win Friends and Influence People*. You won't be sorry. It hasn't sold millions of copies over the past sixty plus years by accident.

Remember, reading is great, but doing is better. If your desire is to be a better oral communicator, I highly recommend you enroll in one or both of the following. Dale Carnegie courses are available in every major city as are Toastmasters International clubs. Both are dedicated to helping develop the skills of those who wish to communicate orally with more confidence and expertise. I can assure you both will be money and time well spent.

When Doing Your Job…Work to Exceed Expectations

One of my mantras for life is "do more than is expected." I have discovered that if you are constantly doing more than is expected, you will never again have to worry about evaluations, regardless of the form or fashion they might take.

As this concept applies to enhancing our communication skills, I suggest you look around and take inventory of the expectations people have of the various communicators in their life. If you are a teacher, pay close attention to other teachers and students. If you are a manager, pay close attention to other managers and employees. If you are a parent, pay close attention to other parents and children. If you are a member of the clergy, pay close attention to other spiritual shepherds and their flocks. Watch and listen. Gather up all the good ideas you can unearth and incorporate them into your communication "bag of tricks." At the same time, notice the communication gaps that exist and that people are talking about. Then do everything you can to make sure you are not guilty of the same.

One other thing. Don't wait for your boss, your spouse, your parent, your client or anyone else to challenge you to exceed their expectations. It probably won't happen. Remember, they aren't expecting much. The opportunity always exists for you to give them more.

When Doing Your Job…Never Give Up

I will make this last point short and sweet. Don't you dare give up! Don't ever allow yourself to be lured into thinking that your effort toward developing your interpersonal communication skills means little. Communicating person-to-person means everything. Where a communication void exists, rumors, assumptions, half-truths and perceptions creep in to fill it. There is no need for that to happen.

Conclusion:

What Does It All Mean?

In the first paragraph of the first chapter of this book I wrote:

Just Another Day

The day dawned like every other day. There were the normal work day things to be done and limited time to do them all. From all outward appearances, this was just one more normal, predictable, chaotic day… None of us could have predicted the lasting memory that would be made that day. And none of us could have imagined the value of the lesson learned from it.

If you have read from that first paragraph to this one, I congratulate you on your diligence and commitment to personal development. I hope you have found value in every page.

As the first paragraph states, the day I encountered Joe's extraordinary doctor "dawned like every other day" for me. And "from all outward appearances" there was nothing exceptional about it. There is no way I "could have predicted the lasting memory that would be made that day," nor could I "have imagined the value of the lesson learned from it." But the fact is, as ordinary as the day might have seemed, I came away from it a changed person for the experience. Because of the example of one pediatric physician, I began the journey to becoming a better communicator that very day.

That is what I wish for every person who reads this book. I wish that their life would be changed and their communication enhanced—at home, at work, at school, at play, everywhere! And I wish that process begins this very day.

Do No Harm

Though not a doctor myself, I understand that every certified physician is required to take the Hippocratic Oath which reminds medical practitioners to first and foremost, "Do no harm."

Harm can come in many forms. Besides physical harm, there can be emotional harm, psychological harm and so on. Without saying so, the doctor who treated my son seemed intent on doing no harm to Joe in any of these areas. Of course, he initially met Joe at a point where physical harm had already occurred. Therefore, the doctor seemed to redouble his efforts to limit the possible emotional harm ("...Because you're special, I'm going to give you 'cat whiskers'..." instead of stitches) and psychological harm ("...these shots are going to hurt—but they won't hurt very long.") thereby working to limit lingering psychological fears of pain associated with doctors, doctor's offices and needles.

If doctor's are required to take a Hippocratic Oath to practice medicine, maybe communicators ought to be required to take a "Lip"pocratic Oath in order to practice one-on-one communication techniques. The mantra, "Do no harm" would still be appropriate. Communicators should always strive to avoid causing harm with their message, their method and the emotions that both can evoke.

Six Principles Revisited

As we move forward from this point, I hope the six principles I watched the doctor practice will serve as foundation stones for your future communication efforts as well. Get in the habit of asking yourself:

- *Have I **talked with people** instead of at them?*

- *Have I taken the time to **explain the process** in advance of the procedure while people's minds are still open and pliable?*

- *Have I **told the truth** today so I can be trusted tomorrow?*

- *Have I dedicated myself to **work for understanding** throughout the communication process?*

- *Have I made every possible effort to **get them involved** in the communication process and all that will follow it?*

- *Have I **done my job** even when that job proved less than pleasurable?*

One Final Wish

I have often fantasized about wandering down an isolated beach and happening upon a barnacle encrusted bottle partially buried in the sand. You know the fable. The finder of the bottle begins to clean and polish it and in so doing releases a genie who has been trapped inside for centuries. Eternally grateful, the genie proceeds to grant three wishes as a means of showing his gratitude.

My fantasy is similar to that of the fable, but with a more updated, 21st century twist. Upon cleaning and polishing my bottle, the genie appears only to show himself much stingier than his counterparts of old.

"Hey, bud. Thanks for springing me from the bottle. It was beginning to cramp my style. HA-HA-HA. Get it? Cramping my style? I have been *cramped* up in that bottle for three hundred and fifty years. Not much of a sense of humor, huh? So you don't appreciate good genie humor?

"Anyway, I owe you. So here's the deal. You get one wish. I know, I know, you were expecting three, everybody does. But times are tough. Haven't you been reading the papers?

"So you get one wish and it's not going to do you any good to wish for a million bucks or for a date with a movie star or any ridiculous wishes like that. I can only grant your wish if it can help both you and others.

"So what'll it be, bud? I don't have all century! Get it? Not a day, a *Century!* Man, you're a tough audience!

Enough of that. But what if there was really one wish available? What would you wish for? I already know what my wish would be.

I would wish for the ability to communicate with literally every person I meet, regardless of age, sex, status, geography, culture – *on their level* – not them on mine. In so doing, I believe most of my other dreams and goals would be realized.

That's what this book was intended to do – to help you realize your dreams and goals – to help you build trust and communicate successfully when the results are critical. But you don't have to wait and wish for such a reality. Start practicing these tips and watch your dreams start coming true – today!

All the best!

About The Author

PHILLIP VAN HOOSER has spoken, written and consulted on leadership development issues worldwide since 1988.

Corporations across the U.S. and around the globe have used Van Hooser's management training system, "The Leadership Journey," and his popular book, "Willie's Way: 6 Secrets for Wooing, Wowing and Winning Customers and Their Loyalty," to help their people develop a renewed spirit for leading their employees and serving their customers.

Phil's perspectives and personal experiences in FORTUNE 500 America change the way people think about leadership and service. A frequent keynote speaker for top domestic and international groups, Van Hooser's clients include the Club Managers Association of America, Blue Bell Creameries, BlueCross BlueShield, Lockheed Martin, KPMG, KeyBank, and El Nacional.

A longtime member of the National Speakers Association, Phil has earned NSA's Certified Speaking Professional designation and is a member of the Speaker Hall of Fame. From 2009 to 2010, Phil served his industry and his colleagues as President of the National Speakers Association.

Phil earned a B.S. in Marketing from Murray State University and holds a Masters in Business Administration from Nova Southeastern University. For more information, please visit www.vanhooser.com.

Willie's Way
6 Secrets for Wooing, Wowing and Winning Customers and Their Loyalty

www.williesway.com

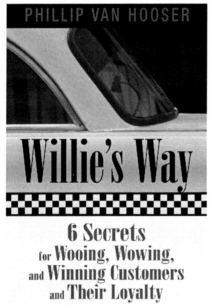

Phillip Van Hooser's real life encounter with a South Carolina cabdriver forever changed how he measured customer service. Most people don't think of a cabdriver as a role model for great customer service. But Van Hooser's account of his experience with Willie proves that great customer service can be delivered even in the most difficult circumstances.

Willie doesn't have an MBA, but he doesn't need one to know that the most critical aspect of salesmanship is a personal relationship with the customer. In fact, people enjoy doing business with people they know and like – and they remember people they like when it's time to do business again. The simple things Willie does to get to know his customers not only leave them happy, but also leave them wanting more of his special brand of service.

What business leader wouldn't want his customers to feel the same way?

This engaging and entertaining book translates Willie's commonsense approach to customer satisfaction into practical applications you can apply in any customer relationship!

You're Joe's boy, ain't ya
Life's Lessons for Living, Loving and Leading

Do you want to live, love and lead with contentment and purpose? In *You're Joe's boy, ain't ya?*, Phillip Van Hooser shares the lessons from life that have helped him – and can help you – build a solid footing in today's rocky world.

His classroom? Life itself. His teachers? Family, friends and folks he's met along the way. The result? Sixteen comforting stories to stir your heart and strengthen your purpose.

Good old fashioned wisdom that will touch your emotions. A delightfully warm, thought provoking book.

The Leadership Journey
Practical Skills for Leadership Development
www.businesstrainingexperts.com

Available on DVD, CD-ROM and Online (web-based) formats, **The Leadership Journey** includes 24 courses that will engage your managers and supervisors while teaching them practical skills they can apply immediately. No more theory based courses that have no practical applications. Twenty minute courses allow managers to learn quickly while spending little time away from the job.

Courses address issues including conflict management, motivating others, coping with change, leadership, professionalism, decision making, empowerment and much more.

A complete training system, **The Leadership Journey** includes video presentation with PowerPoint, Pre and Post Training Questions, Discussion Questions, Facilitator's Guide, Student Materials, Pre and Post Training Testing, Tracking and Role Play Exercises.

About The Illustrator

KEVIN VANHOOSER is an illustration alumnus of the College for Creative Studies in Detroit. His work covers a broad spectrum of subjects, from the sports world all the way to still life and landscape. Working in various mediums his passion is with oils. As an illustrator, his goal is to tell a story with his own language while creating an image. While still young in "artist years", Kevin worked for a small Chicago area sports publication. He has also shown work at various galleries in and around the Detroit area including the Detroit Artist Market. His work can be viewed online at www.kvanhooser.com, and he can be contacted directly at kevinvanhooser@gmail.com.